Understanding Trust Structures

A Governance Framework Guide

A Plain-Language Introduction to Trust Structure,
Revocable & Irrevocable Frameworks,
& Educational Trust Templates

J.B MORENO

Prepared by:
J.B. Moreno

Version: First Edition, 2026
Date: February 2026

Understanding comes first. Decisions can wait.

DISCLAIMER

This guide is provided for educational and informational purposes only.

It explains structural concepts related to trust architecture and governance design. It does not provide legal, tax, financial, or investment advice.

Trust classification, enforceability, tax treatment, and regulatory considerations vary by jurisdiction and circumstance. Implementation of any trust structure requires careful drafting and alignment with applicable law.

Nothing in this guide should be interpreted as a substitute for individualized professional counsel.

Readers are responsible for seeking qualified advice before executing or relying upon any legal instrument.

TABLE OF CONTENTS

FRONT MATTER

PART I — FOUNDATIONS OF TRUST ARCHITECTURE

PART II — TRUST STRUCTURE CATEGORIES

PART III — CORE FRAMEWORK ANALYSIS

PART IV — STRUCTURAL ILLUSTRATIONS

APPENDICES

CLOSING

INTRODUCTION

Trusts are often presented in fragmented or highly technical language. This guide was written to provide structural clarity.

It explains how trust frameworks are organized, how governance roles function, and how architectural decisions influence long-term administration.

This book presents:

- An educational overview of trust concepts

- Structural explanations of common trust models

- Illustrative clause frameworks for learning

- Narrative examples to reinforce architecture

The purpose of this guide is clarity — not urgency.

Understanding precedes implementation.

HOW TO USE THIS GUIDE

This guide is structured progressively.

Readers may approach it in one of three ways.

Sequential Review

Recommended for first-time readers. Begin with foundational architecture, proceed to framework comparisons, and conclude with structural applications.

Topic-Based Review

Readers with familiarity may navigate directly to trust categories, governance models, or illustrative examples.

Reference Review

This guide may also function as a structural reference for revisiting trustee roles, distribution philosophy, or architectural distinctions.

Each section is designed to stand independently while reinforcing the broader framework.

No immediate decision is required.

Structural clarity precedes implementation.

SECTION 1 — CHOOSING A TRUST FRAMEWORK

(Revocable vs. Irrevocable — Structural Overview)

Why This Section Exists

Many readers encounter the terms *revocable* and *irrevocable* before fully understanding what they mean. That exposure can create unnecessary pressure to choose prematurely.

This section removes that pressure.

Both frameworks are presented to support comparison and reflection. No selection is required to continue.

Two Frameworks, Two Structural Approaches

Trusts are commonly organized using one of two structural models:

- Revocable Trust Framework
- Irrevocable Trust Framework

The distinction centers on retained authority and permanence — not complexity.

Neither framework is inherently superior. Each reflects a different governance intention.

The Revocable Trust Framework

A revocable trust emphasizes flexibility.

Within this framework:

- The trust may be amended
- Assets may be added or removed
- Terms may evolve
- The trust may be revoked during the grantor's lifetime

Its defining characteristic is retained authority within a documented structure.

The Irrevocable Trust Framework

An irrevocable trust emphasizes structural permanence.

Within this framework:

- Amendment authority is limited
- Roles are intentionally separated
- Retained control is reduced
- Long-term governance stability is prioritized

Its defining characteristic is restricted modification and defined independence.

A Practical Distinction

A simple structural summary:

A revocable trust retains amendment authority.
An irrevocable trust is designed to operate as written.

The difference lies in control — not sophistication.

Common Contexts for Exploration

Revocable trusts are often examined when flexibility and lifetime control are priorities.

Irrevocable trusts are often examined when governance independence and long-term structure are emphasized.

These are structural observations — not recommendations.

No Immediate Decision Required

Understanding precedes implementation.

You may review both frameworks, compare their structural implications, and revisit this section as needed. No selection is required before continuing.

Professional Orientation

Trust structures — particularly irrevocable ones — can carry lasting legal and financial implications.

This guide presents architecture for understanding. Professional review is appropriate before implementation.

SECTION 2 — UNDERSTANDING: WHAT A TRUST IS

(Conceptual Foundation)

What a Trust Is — Before Legal Terminology

The word *trust* often carries assumptions of complexity.

A trust is a structured legal relationship.

It defines:

- Who establishes the arrangement
- Who manages assets
- Who benefits
- Under what conditions

The written document records this structure. It does not create complexity — it creates clarity.

A Practical Analogy

A trust is a structured container governed by defined rules.

Assets are placed within it.
Authority and benefit are assigned according to written terms.

The trust is not a person.
It is a framework for managing property under defined conditions.

The Three Core Roles

(The Foundation of Every Trust)

Every trust — regardless of complexity — revolves around three roles.

1. The Grantor (Settlor)

The grantor:

- Establishes the trust
- Defines its purpose
- Sets its initial terms
- Transfers assets into it

This role originates the structure.

---

2. The Trustee

The trustee:

- Administers the trust
- Manages trust assets
- Follows written instructions
- Acts in a fiduciary capacity

The trustee manages property but does not own it personally.

---

3. The Beneficiaries

Beneficiaries:

- Receive benefits from the trust
- May receive income or distributions
- Do not automatically control administration

The trust exists for their benefit according to its written terms.

Why Role Structure Matters

Trust outcomes depend on how these roles are arranged.

Sometimes one individual occupies multiple roles.
Sometimes roles are intentionally separated.
Sometimes authority shifts over time.

Structure determines control, flexibility, and continuity.

Ownership vs. Control

Trusts allow ownership, control, and benefit to be separated.

An individual may:

- No longer personally own an asset
- Still influence administration
- Or benefit under defined standards

This separation is a defining feature of trust design.

What a Trust Is Not

A trust is not:

- A guarantee of tax reduction
- A method to avoid legal obligations
- A universal solution
- A substitute for professional advice

Trusts are governance tools — not shortcuts.

Historical Purpose

Trusts developed historically to:

- Manage property across generations
- Preserve continuity
- Reduce disputes
- Carry out long-term intent

Modern trust structures serve the same function: structured continuity across time.

Understanding Before Implementation

Understanding architecture enables informed participation in professional discussions — without requiring immediate action.

Everything that follows builds on this foundation.

SECTION 3 — STRUCTURAL ORGANIZATION OF THIS GUIDE

(Foundational and Expanded Frameworks)

Why This Organizational Model Is Included

Trust structures vary in complexity.

Some emphasize core mechanics and clarity.
Others introduce layered governance and expanded administrative provisions.

This guide presents trust architecture in progressive depth to help readers understand how structure evolves without losing coherence.

The purpose of this sequencing is comparison — not recommendation.

Foundational Structure

The foundational framework illustrates core trust mechanics, including:

- Role identification
- Basic governance language
- Standard asset coordination
- Clear administrative structure

This level emphasizes architectural clarity.

It demonstrates how a trust functions at its most essential level.

Expanded Structural Layer

The expanded framework builds upon foundational elements by incorporating:

- Additional trustee provisions
- Broader administrative authority
- Contingency planning structures
- Clarified distribution standards

This layer demonstrates how governance language becomes more detailed while preserving structural integrity.

Specialized Adaptations

Some trust structures introduce further adaptation depending on asset type or planning objective.

Examples may include:

- Asset-specific governance provisions
- Multi-layer trustee succession models
- Defined discretion standards
- Protective or conditional clauses

These adaptations expand upon foundational architecture.
They do not replace it.

How to Read This Progression

Readers may:

- Begin with foundational concepts and progress toward expanded models
- Compare structural depth across examples
- Revisit earlier sections as complexity increases

Understanding architectural progression makes trust documents easier to interpret in practice.

Structural Reminder

This organizational model is presented for educational clarity.

Actual implementation depends on jurisdiction, drafting precision, execution requirements, and professional review.

SECTION 4 — TRUST ARCHITECTURE

(How Trusts Are Structured and How the Pieces Interact)

Why Trust Architecture Matters

Once you understand what a trust is and how foundational frameworks differ, the next question becomes:

How is a trust actually built?

Trust architecture refers to how roles, authority, and responsibility are arranged within a structure. Like a building, a trust may be simple or layered — but unclear structure produces future friction.

Architecture determines durability.

A Trust as a Blueprint

A trust functions as a blueprint for governance.

It answers questions such as:

- Who is authorized to act?
- Who steps in if authority shifts?
- How are decisions evaluated?
- Who ultimately benefits?

Good architecture eliminates assumption.
It relies on written clarity.

Core Structural Roles (Applied)

Trust architecture centers on role coordination.

Grantor

The grantor establishes the structure, defines its purpose, and transfers property into it.

The grantor is not automatically the trustee.
The grantor is not always a beneficiary.
Role overlap is possible — but it is a design choice.

Trustee

The trustee administers the trust pursuant to written terms.

This includes:

- Managing trust property
- Acting in good faith
- Maintaining records
- Making distributions as authorized

The trustee manages assets.
The trustee does not own them personally.

This distinction prevents confusion between control and ownership.

Successor Trustee

A successor trustee ensures continuity.

If the acting trustee resigns, becomes incapacitated, or is unable to serve, the successor assumes responsibility pursuant to defined terms.

Trusts are designed for continuity.
Succession planning prevents interruption.

Beneficiaries

Beneficiaries receive benefit according to defined standards.

They do not automatically control administration.

Being a beneficiary does not equate to managerial authority.

Ownership and Control

Trust design allows ownership, control, and benefit to be intentionally separated.

An individual may:

- Relinquish direct title
- Retain defined authority
- Or receive benefit under structured conditions

This separation is a structural tool — not an accident.

Trusts and Wills — Coordinated, Not Identical

A will governs probate assets and directs distribution at death.

A trust governs assets associated with it during life or through structured transfer.

In many planning structures, the two documents coordinate rather than substitute for one another.

A trust does not automatically eliminate the need for a will.

Funding and Asset Alignment

Creating a trust document does not automatically transfer assets into it.

For a trust to govern property, assets must be formally aligned with the structure in accordance with applicable law and institutional procedure.

This process is commonly referred to as funding.

Funding may involve:

- Retitling property
- Assigning ownership interests
- Updating beneficiary designations
- Executing transfer instruments

The trust establishes architecture.
Funding aligns assets with that architecture.

Without proper alignment, a trust may exist while certain assets remain outside its governance.

Because asset alignment varies by jurisdiction and asset type, professional coordination is often appropriate.

Architecture Evolves Across Time

Trusts are frequently designed to operate differently across stages:

- During lifetime
- Upon incapacity
- Upon death

Role transitions and authority shifts are defined in advance.

Understanding architecture enables readers to interpret trust documents with clarity rather than intimidation.

Purpose of This Section

The goal is not memorization.

It is to help you:

- Recognize structural roles
- Understand how authority is arranged
- Interpret trust language confidently
- Ask informed questions when appropriate

Everything that follows builds on this architectural framework.

SECTION 5 — FOUNDATIONAL TRUST STRUCTURES

(Primary Governance Models)

Purpose of This Section

This section examines foundational trust structures organized primarily by timing, beneficiary design, and governance intent.

Each structure applies the architectural principles introduced in earlier sections.
While the underlying mechanics of trusts remain consistent, governance objectives vary.

Some structures emphasize flexibility.
Others emphasize sequencing, protection, or long-term continuity.

Understanding these distinctions clarifies how purpose shapes design.

Structural Orientation

The trust types presented in this section are categorized as foundational because they:

- Represent commonly referenced trust frameworks
- Establish baseline governance models
- Serve as structural building blocks for more specialized adaptations
- Illustrate how beneficiary design influences administration

These models are not mutually exclusive.
A single trust instrument may incorporate elements from multiple foundational categories.

Educational Scope

The descriptions that follow are structural in nature.

They:

- Explain governance mechanics
- Clarify role interaction
- Highlight distribution philosophy
- Illustrate administrative orientation

They do not prescribe implementation, predict legal outcomes, or replace professional drafting.

Trust classification, tax treatment, enforceability, and regulatory considerations depend on jurisdiction and document precision.

This section provides structural literacy only.

Transition

Each foundational structure below should be read through the lens of architecture:

Who controls?
Who benefits?
When does authority shift?
How is continuity preserved?

The answers to those questions define the structure.

GRANTOR VS. NON-GRANTOR

(Educational Structural Overview)

What This Classification Focuses On

Trusts may be distinguished not only by structural design (revocable or irrevocable), but also by income tax classification.

The terms *grantor trust* and *non-grantor trust* describe how a trust is treated for income tax purposes.
They do not describe the legal validity of the trust itself.

This distinction affects reporting and tax responsibility — not core architecture.

What a Grantor Trust Is

A grantor trust is generally treated, for income tax purposes, as owned by the individual who created it.

In conceptual terms:

- Trust income is typically reported by the grantor
- The trust may not function as a separate taxable entity during the grantor's lifetime
- Certain retained powers may influence classification

Many revocable trusts are treated as grantor trusts.
Some irrevocable trusts may also qualify depending on retained authority.

Grantor status reflects tax treatment, not structural simplicity.

What a Non-Grantor Trust Is

A non-grantor trust is generally treated as a separate taxable entity.

In such structures:

- The trust may obtain its own tax identification number
- Income may be reported at the trust level
- Distributions may carry tax implications for beneficiaries

Non-grantor classification does not inherently imply asset protection, permanence, or distribution style.
It is a reporting distinction.

Retained Powers and Classification

Tax classification often depends on whether the grantor retains specific powers, such as:

- The power to revoke
- The power to amend
- The power to substitute assets
- The power to control beneficial enjoyment

Retention of certain powers may result in grantor treatment.
Limitation of those powers may result in non-grantor treatment.

Because classification depends on statutory frameworks and drafting precision, professional review is essential.

Relationship to Other Trust Types

Grantor vs. non-grantor classification:

- Crosses both revocable and irrevocable frameworks
- Does not determine distribution philosophy
- Does not define beneficiary structure
- Does not dictate trustee independence

It is a tax overlay applied to structural architecture.

Common Misunderstandings

This classification is sometimes misunderstood as:

- A structural label
- An asset protection designation
- A measure of trust complexity
- A standalone planning objective

In reality, it describes how income is taxed — not how authority is arranged.

Educational Illustration (Fictional)

A fictional individual establishes an irrevocable trust but retains specific substitution powers permitted under applicable law. As a result, the trust may be treated as a grantor trust for income tax purposes despite its irrevocable structure.

This illustrates how classification and structure are related but not identical.

How This Classification Fits Within This Guide

Grantor vs. non-grantor status is categorized as foundational because:

- It frequently appears in planning discussions
- It intersects with both revocable and irrevocable frameworks
- It influences reporting obligations

Understanding this distinction strengthens structural literacy without conflating tax treatment with governance design.

LIVING TRUST

(Educational Overview)

What This Trust Type Focuses On

A Living Trust is created during an individual's lifetime to hold, manage, and distribute assets according to defined written terms.

It is widely referenced as a foundational planning structure because of its administrative continuity and structural flexibility.

Living trusts are commonly organized in two primary forms:

- Revocable Living Trust
- Irrevocable Living Trust

This overview describes structure, not jurisdiction-specific outcomes.

What a Living Trust Is

A living trust establishes a legal relationship among defined parties for the purpose of managing property.

A typical structure includes:

- A grantor (settlor)
- A trustee
- One or more beneficiaries
- Trust-associated property

The trust operates as an administrative framework during life and may continue through incapacity and after death, depending on its design.

Why Living Trusts Are Commonly Explored

Living trusts are often examined because they may:

- Centralize asset administration
- Provide continuity in the event of incapacity
- Clarify distribution instructions
- Reduce reliance on court-supervised proceedings in certain circumstances
- Preserve administrative privacy compared to some public processes

For many individuals, a living trust functions as a structural foundation upon which additional planning mechanisms may be built.

Revocable Living Trust (Conceptual Overview)

A revocable living trust emphasizes flexibility and retained authority.

Common characteristics include:

- Ability to amend or restate terms
- Ability to add or remove assets
- Ability to modify trustee or beneficiary designations
- Ability to revoke the trust entirely

Because authority is typically retained, revocable living trusts are frequently discussed in the context of personal organization and continuity planning.

Irrevocable Living Trust (Conceptual Overview)

An irrevocable living trust emphasizes defined structure and reduced retained control.

Common characteristics include:

- Limited ability to modify terms
- Greater separation between grantor and trust property
- Defined administrative boundaries
- Reliance on trustee authority as written

Irrevocable structures are typically evaluated in more specialized planning contexts involving permanence and long-term governance.

The distinction between revocable and irrevocable forms may influence control, taxation, and administration, but outcomes depend on structure and jurisdiction.

Common Assets Held in Living Trusts

Living trusts may hold:

- Real property
- Financial and investment accounts
- Business or personal property interests

Assets must be properly aligned with the trust to fall under its administration.

Administration Considerations

Effective administration generally involves:

- Maintaining accurate records
- Managing assets under fiduciary standards
- Following written distribution terms
- Planning for successor trusteeship
- Coordinating with financial institutions and counterparties

Clarity in drafting supports continuity in administration.

Common Misunderstandings

Living trusts are sometimes misunderstood as:

- Automatically eliminating taxes
- Replacing all legal processes
- Operating without administrative oversight

They are organizational governance tools. Outcomes depend on structure and implementation.

Educational Illustration (Fictional)

A fictional individual establishes a revocable living trust to centralize real property, financial accounts, and personal assets within a single administrative structure. During lifetime, the grantor serves as trustee and retains amendment authority. The trust designates a successor trustee to assume management in the event of incapacity or death.

This example illustrates structural continuity — not legal outcomes.

How Living Trusts Fit Within This Guide

Living trusts are categorized as foundational because they:

- Appear frequently in planning discussions
- Provide a baseline structural model
- Serve as a platform for more specialized adaptations

Subsequent sections explore purpose-driven and asset-specific structures that build upon or diverge from this foundational form.

TESTAMENTARY TRUST

(Educational Overview)

What This Trust Type Focuses On

A Testamentary Trust is created through a will and becomes effective upon the death of the individual who executed it.

Unlike living trusts, it does not operate during the grantor's lifetime.

This overview describes structure and timing, not jurisdiction-specific procedure or outcomes.

What a Testamentary Trust Is

A testamentary trust is established by provisions written into a valid will. The trust does not function independently until the triggering event — typically death — occurs.

Once activated, the trust:

- Is formally recognized
- Receives assets as directed by the will
- Is administered by a trustee for designated beneficiaries

Because it originates within a will, its formation is commonly associated with court-supervised estate administration.

Why Testamentary Trusts Are Commonly Explored

Testamentary trusts are often examined because they may:

- Provide structured distribution after death
- Delay or condition beneficiary access
- Offer oversight for minors or dependents
- Centralize post-death asset management under defined terms
- Integrate trust provisions within a single testamentary instrument

They are typically considered when lifetime administration is unnecessary or not desired.

How Testamentary Trusts Differ from Living Trusts

Key structural distinctions include:

Timing
Testamentary trusts become effective after death.
Living trusts operate during lifetime.

Method of Creation
Testamentary trusts arise from a will.
Living trusts are created through separate trust instruments.

Administrative Path
Testamentary trusts are generally formed as part of estate administration.
Living trusts may operate independently during life.

These differences influence continuity, privacy, and administrative sequencing.

Common Assets Held in Testamentary Trusts

Assets directed into testamentary trusts may include:

- Real property
- Financial accounts or investment proceeds
- Estate-distributed assets

Transfer occurs as part of estate administration.

Administration Considerations

Administration commonly involves:

- Appointment or confirmation of a trustee
- Compliance with fiduciary obligations
- Possible reporting or procedural requirements
- Distribution according to written standards

Because the trust arises after death, administration follows formal sequencing defined by applicable law and the governing instrument.

Common Misunderstandings

Testamentary trusts are sometimes misunderstood as:

- Operating during lifetime
- Avoiding all court involvement
- Functioning identically to living trusts

They are post-death governance structures activated through a will.

Educational Illustration (Fictional)

A fictional individual includes provisions in a will directing that specified assets be placed into a trust for the benefit of a minor child. Upon death, the trust is established, a trustee is appointed, and assets are administered until the beneficiary reaches defined milestones.

This example illustrates structured sequencing — not legal outcomes.

How Testamentary Trusts Fit Within This Guide

Testamentary trusts are categorized as foundational because they:

- Represent a traditional trust mechanism
- Provide a baseline comparison to living trusts
- Illustrate timing-based trust creation

Understanding testamentary trusts clarifies how lifetime and post-death structures differ in governance design.

FAMILY TRUST

(Educational Overview)

What This Trust Type Focuses On

A Family Trust is structured to manage and distribute assets for the benefit of defined family members under written governance standards.

It is frequently associated with intergenerational planning, coordinated asset administration, and long-term continuity.

A family trust may be structured as revocable or irrevocable depending on planning intent.

This overview addresses structural purpose, not jurisdiction-specific outcomes.

What a Family Trust Is

A family trust is not a single standardized legal form.
It is a purpose-driven arrangement in which beneficiaries are members of a defined family group.

A typical structure includes:

- A grantor
- A trustee (individual or institutional)
- Family beneficiaries
- Designated trust property

The defining feature is beneficiary scope and governance intent — not timing alone.

Why Family Trusts Are Commonly Explored

Family trusts are often examined because they may:

- Coordinate asset management across generations
- Establish consistent distribution standards
- Provide oversight for minors or dependents
- Centralize fiduciary administration
- Preserve clarity of intent over time

They are frequently discussed in contexts where continuity and structured stewardship are priorities.

Relationship to Other Foundational Structures

A family trust may overlap with other foundational forms:

- A living trust may function as a family trust during lifetime.
- A testamentary trust may establish a family trust upon death.
- A marital trust may operate within a broader family trust framework.

The term "family trust" generally describes purpose and beneficiary alignment rather than creation method.

Common Assets Held in Family Trusts

Family trusts may hold:

- Real property
- Investment portfolios
- Business or generational assets

Asset selection often reflects preservation and coordinated distribution objectives.

Administration Considerations

Effective administration commonly includes:

- Applying fiduciary standards impartially
- Managing potential conflicts among beneficiaries
- Maintaining accurate records
- Following distribution standards
- Planning for trustee succession

Because multiple beneficiaries are involved, clarity in governance design is essential.

Common Misunderstandings

Family trusts are sometimes misunderstood as:

- Informal family arrangements
- Guaranteed conflict-prevention tools
- Uniform structures suitable for all families

They require disciplined drafting and administration.

Educational Illustration (Fictional)

A fictional individual establishes a trust to hold investment assets and real property for the benefit of children and future descendants. The trustee administers assets under defined distribution standards emphasizing health, education, maintenance, and support. Successor trustees are designated to ensure continuity beyond the grantor's lifetime.

This example illustrates structured family-focused governance — not legal outcomes.

How Family Trusts Fit Within This Guide

Family trusts are categorized as foundational because they:

- Appear frequently in estate and generational planning discussions
- Build upon living and testamentary trust concepts
- Provide a base model for coordinated beneficiary governance

Understanding family trust structure clarifies how long-term stewardship may be embedded within trust architecture.

MARITAL / QTIP TRUST

(Educational Overview)

What This Trust Type Focuses On

A Marital Trust is structured to provide financial benefit to a surviving spouse while defining how trust assets are distributed thereafter.

One commonly referenced variation is the Qualified Terminable Interest Property (QTIP) trust, which allows lifetime benefit to a spouse while preserving control over ultimate distribution.

This overview addresses structural sequencing and governance intent. It does not assume jurisdiction, tax treatment, or specific legal outcomes.

What a Marital / QTIP Trust Is

A marital trust is a trust arrangement that:

- Provides defined benefit to a surviving spouse during their lifetime
- Establishes remainder beneficiaries who receive assets afterward

A QTIP-style structure emphasizes terminable interest — meaning the spouse may receive income or defined benefit but does not control final disposition.

A typical structure includes:

- A grantor
- A trustee
- A surviving spouse as primary lifetime beneficiary
- Remainder beneficiaries designated for future distribution

The defining characteristic is sequenced beneficial interest rather than joint ownership.

Why Marital / QTIP Trusts Are Commonly Explored

These structures are often examined because they may:

- Provide lifetime financial support to a surviving spouse
- Preserve principal for designated remainder beneficiaries
- Coordinate planning in blended family contexts
- Clarify long-term inheritance intent
- Balance present support with future preservation

They are frequently discussed where multiple beneficiary interests must be aligned over time.

Structural Sequencing

Marital trusts are distinguished by layered benefit:

During the Spouse's Lifetime

- Income may be distributed pursuant to defined standards
- Principal access may be limited or governed by trustee discretion
- Trustee neutrality between present and future interests is essential

Upon the Spouse's Passing

- Remaining assets pass to designated remainder beneficiaries
- Distribution follows the grantor's written sequencing
- Ownership does not reclassify during the spouse's lifetime

The structure formalizes staged transition rather than unrestricted transfer.

Common Assets Held in Marital / QTIP Trusts

Marital trusts may hold:

- Income-producing investment assets
- Real property
- Preservation-oriented principal assets

Asset selection often reflects income generation balanced with remainder protection.

Administration Considerations

Effective administration commonly includes:

- Managing income distributions
- Preserving principal consistent with remainder design
- Maintaining fiduciary neutrality
- Planning for trustee succession
- Coordinating with broader estate structure

Because dual beneficiary interests exist, clarity in drafting and trustee authority is critical.

Common Misunderstandings

Marital and QTIP trusts are sometimes misunderstood as:

- Granting full ownership to the surviving spouse
- Eliminating long-term planning
- Functioning as joint ownership substitutes

They are sequencing tools — not ownership transfers.

Educational Illustration (Fictional)

A fictional individual establishes a trust providing lifetime income to a surviving spouse while directing that remaining principal pass to children from a prior relationship. The trustee administers assets under defined standards, balancing current support with remainder preservation.

This example illustrates structured layering of beneficiary interests — not tax or legal outcomes.

How Marital / QTIP Trusts Fit Within This Guide

Marital and QTIP trusts are categorized as foundational because they:

- Represent a common sequencing model in estate planning
- Build upon living and family trust frameworks
- Illustrate layered beneficiary governance

Understanding these structures clarifies how lifetime support and future distribution may be coordinated within trust architecture.

How Marital / QTIP Trusts Fit Within This Guide

SPENDTHRIFT TRUST

(Educational Overview)

What This Trust Type Focuses On

A Spendthrift Trust is structured to limit a beneficiary's ability to transfer, assign, or prematurely access trust assets.

Its defining feature is restricted beneficiary control combined with trustee oversight.

Spendthrift provisions may exist as:

- A standalone trust structure, or
- A protective clause embedded within another trust

This overview addresses governance design. It does not assume enforceability in any specific jurisdiction.

What a Spendthrift Trust Is

A spendthrift trust is characterized by separation between beneficiary benefit and beneficiary control.

Common structural features include:

- Assets held and administered by a trustee
- Restrictions on voluntary or involuntary transfer of beneficiary interests
- Limited direct access to principal
- Trustee-controlled distribution authority

The central mechanism is fiduciary management in place of beneficiary ownership authority.

Why Spendthrift Trusts Are Commonly Explored

These structures are often examined because they may:

- Promote measured distribution over time
- Support beneficiaries requiring financial oversight
- Limit direct beneficiary control
- Reinforce disciplined administration
- Preserve trust assets for defined purposes

They are generally associated with controlled access rather than unrestricted entitlement.

Relationship to Other Foundational Structures

Spendthrift provisions frequently operate within broader trust frameworks:

- A family trust may incorporate spendthrift protections
- A testamentary trust may apply spendthrift restrictions to inherited assets
- A living trust may activate spendthrift provisions upon succession

In many cases, "spendthrift trust" describes a functional protection feature rather than an entirely separate trust category.

Common Assets Held in Spendthrift Trusts

Spendthrift trusts may hold:

- Investment accounts
- Income-producing property
- Financial reserves designated for structured distribution

Asset selection aligns with preservation and oversight objectives.

Administration Considerations

Administration typically involves:

- Trustee discretion within defined standards
- Ongoing fiduciary evaluation of beneficiary needs
- Recordkeeping and reporting
- Preservation of principal
- Compliance with applicable legal limitations

Because beneficiary authority is limited, trustee selection and clarity of distribution standards are particularly significant.

Common Misunderstandings

Spendthrift trusts are sometimes misunderstood as:

- Absolute protection from all creditors
- Self-settled asset protection mechanisms
- Structures that eliminate fiduciary responsibility

They are governance tools operating within legal limits.

Educational Illustration (Fictional)

A fictional individual establishes a trust for an adult beneficiary with defined distribution standards. The trustee retains discretion over timing and amounts of distributions. The beneficiary cannot assign or pledge their interest in the trust.

This example illustrates restricted access and fiduciary oversight — not guaranteed protection outcomes.

How Spendthrift Trusts Fit Within This Guide

Spendthrift trusts are categorized as foundational because they:

- Represent a core protective governance concept
- Frequently appear within broader trust structures
- Illustrate the separation of benefit and control

Understanding spendthrift principles clarifies how restriction-based governance is incorporated into trust design.

How Spendthrift Trusts Fit Within This Guide

CHARITABLE TRUSTS

(Educational Overview)

What This Trust Type Focuses On

A Charitable Trust is structured to support defined charitable purposes under formal fiduciary administration.

It is commonly discussed in contexts involving philanthropy, public benefit, and long-term mission alignment.

Two frequently referenced conceptual variations include:

- Charitable Remainder Trust (CRT)
- Charitable Lead Trust (CLT)

This overview addresses structural sequencing and purpose orientation. It does not assume tax qualification, regulatory recognition, or jurisdiction-specific treatment.

What a Charitable Trust Is

A charitable trust is a trust arrangement in which one or more charitable organizations are designated beneficiaries either immediately or in the future.

A typical structure includes:

- A grantor
- A trustee
- One or more charitable beneficiaries
- Defined distribution terms aligned with stated purpose

The defining characteristic is public or mission-oriented benefit rather than private beneficiary entitlement.

Charitable trusts may be established during lifetime or through testamentary provisions.

Charitable Remainder Trust (CRT) — Conceptual Overview

A Charitable Remainder Trust is structured so that:

- Non-charitable beneficiaries receive income or defined benefit for a period, and
- Remaining trust assets ultimately pass to a charitable organization

Its distinguishing feature is the remainder interest reserved for charitable use after other beneficial interests conclude.

Charitable Lead Trust (CLT) — Conceptual Overview

A Charitable Lead Trust is structured so that:

- A charitable organization receives benefit first, and
- Remaining trust assets later pass to non-charitable beneficiaries

Its defining feature is the lead interest, which prioritizes charitable distribution during the initial trust term.

Why Charitable Trusts Are Commonly Explored

These structures are often examined because they may:

- Formalize philanthropic objectives
- Provide structured charitable distributions over time
- Align personal or family values with governance design
- Coordinate charitable intent within broader estate planning

They are frequently discussed where private planning intersects with public benefit.

Relationship to Other Foundational Structures

Charitable trusts may operate independently or within broader frameworks:

- A living trust may incorporate charitable provisions
- A testamentary trust may establish charitable distributions
- A family trust may allocate a portion of assets to mission-based purposes

Charitable trusts are distinguished by beneficiary purpose rather than timing alone.

Common Assets Held in Charitable Trusts

Charitable trusts may hold:

- Cash and investment accounts
- Appreciated assets
- Income-producing property

Asset selection often reflects sustainability and distribution timing.

Administration Considerations

Administration commonly includes:

- Adherence to defined charitable purpose
- Fiduciary oversight of distributions
- Recordkeeping and reporting
- Coordination with charitable beneficiaries
- Compliance with applicable legal requirements

Because charitable interests are involved, clarity of intent and documentation is particularly significant.

Common Misunderstandings

Charitable trusts are sometimes misunderstood as:

- Automatically generating tax benefits
- Applicable only to large estates
- Informal donation vehicles

They are formal governance structures aligned with defined charitable purpose.

Educational Illustration (Fictional)

A fictional individual establishes a trust that distributes a defined percentage of investment income annually to a designated charitable organization. The trustee administers assets according to written standards, balancing distribution timing with long-term sustainability.

This example illustrates structured mission alignment — not tax or legal outcomes.

How Charitable Trusts Fit Within This Guide

Charitable trusts are categorized as foundational because they:

- Represent a primary category of purpose-driven trust planning
- Illustrate beneficiary sequencing concepts
- Provide structural models for mission-oriented governance

Understanding charitable trust architecture clarifies how philanthropic intent may be embedded within broader trust frameworks.

SECTION 6 — SPECIALIZED & ASSET-SPECIFIC TRUST STRUCTURES

(Structural Adaptations by Asset Class)

Purpose of This Section

Section 5 examined foundational trust structures organized by timing and beneficiary design.

This section shifts focus.

Here, trust architecture is examined through the lens of asset type.

While the legal mechanics of a trust remain consistent, certain asset categories introduce distinct administrative considerations. These considerations influence governance design, succession planning, and structural coordination.

The objective is not to create new categories of trust law.

It is to demonstrate how established trust principles are applied when assets require heightened coordination, documentation awareness, or continuity planning.

Structural Distinction

Foundational trusts are organized by purpose and beneficiary scope.

Asset-specific trusts are organized by what they hold.

The architecture remains familiar:

- Grantor
- Trustee
- Beneficiaries
- Defined authority

What changes is the context in which those roles operate.

Some assets:

- Require coordination with regulatory systems
- Depend on contractual or platform governance
- Involve licensing or compliance frameworks
- Operate within business or institutional structures

When asset characteristics change, administration changes.

Structure adapts accordingly.

Governance Orientation

The trust types in this section illustrate how:

- Ownership may be separated from operational control
- Compliance considerations influence trustee authority
- Intangible rights require documented oversight
- Succession planning intersects with external systems

These trusts are not new legal inventions.
They are structural applications of existing trust principles to specific asset environments.

Understanding that distinction prevents over-complication.

Educational Scope

The entries that follow:

- Describe governance mechanics
- Highlight administrative distinctions
- Clarify role coordination
- Emphasize structural awareness

They do not provide technical instruction, regulatory guidance, or implementation procedure.

Execution, classification, and enforceability depend on jurisdiction and asset context.

This section provides structural orientation only.

Transition

As you review the following structures, observe:

How does the asset influence trustee responsibility?
Where does external regulation intersect with governance?
What continuity risks does the trust attempt to address?

The answers reveal why architecture must sometimes adapt to asset type.

DIGITAL ASSET / CRYPTO TRUST

(Educational Overview)

What This Trust Type Focuses On

A Digital Asset Trust applies traditional trust architecture to assets that exist primarily within digital systems.

Unlike tangible property, digital assets often rely on access credentials, platform governance, or cryptographic control rather than physical possession. This distinction does not alter core trust principles — but it does influence how authority, succession, and continuity are structured.

Digital assets may include:

- Cryptographic tokens or digital currencies
- Blockchain-based assets
- Platform-based digital property rights
- Credential-dependent access interests

The focus here is structural coordination — not technical management.

Why These Trusts Are Explored

Digital assets introduce administrative challenges that differ from traditional property.

They may:

- Depend on private credentials or authentication systems
- Operate outside traditional financial institutions
- Require documented access continuity
- Become inaccessible if authority transitions are unclear

A trust structure provides documented role alignment and succession planning. It does not change how the asset functions — it clarifies who is authorized to manage it.

Structure Over Technology

This section addresses governance — not acquisition, storage, or cybersecurity.

It does not explain:

- How to purchase digital assets
- How to secure private keys
- How to access specific platforms

Those matters are technical and platform-specific.

The trust framework remains legally architectural.

Role Coordination in a Digital Context

The same roles apply:

- Grantor
- Trustee
- Beneficiaries
- Successor Trustees

What differs is the sensitivity of access continuity.

Where digital assets rely on knowledge-based control, trustee succession and documentation clarity become especially important.

Trust structure provides formal coordination of that authority.

Common Asset Orientation

Digital asset trusts may hold:

- Tokenized financial assets
- Platform-based holdings
- Digitally native property interests

Asset classification and regulatory treatment depend on governing law and platform structure.

What This Trust Type Is Not

A digital asset trust is not:

- A security protocol
- A technical instruction manual
- A guaranteed access solution
- A tax strategy

It is a governance framework applied to digitally administered assets.

Framework Flexibility

Digital assets may be administered within either:

- Revocable frameworks (flexible coordination)
- Irrevocable frameworks (structured separation)

The architectural model depends on governance objectives — not the asset's digital nature.

Key Takeaway

A digital asset trust does not redefine trust law.

It applies established trust principles to assets that depend on documented access, authority coordination, and continuity planning.

Structure remains constant.
Context changes.

LAND TRUST

(Educational Overview)

What This Trust Type Focuses On

A Land Trust is a trust structure used to hold title to real property under defined administrative authority.

Unlike broader living or family trusts that may hold multiple asset categories, a land trust is typically organized around real estate ownership and title administration.

The trust framework separates record title from beneficial interest, creating a structured layer of ownership governance.

Why Land Trusts Are Explored

Land trusts are commonly examined where:

- Privacy of ownership is a consideration
- Title continuity is desired
- Multiple beneficial interests require coordination
- Real property administration benefits from centralized authority

The trust does not alter property law.
It provides a documented structure for holding and administering title.

Structural Orientation

In a typical land trust:

- The trustee holds legal title to the property
- Beneficiaries retain defined beneficial interests
- Authority is exercised according to written trust terms

Operational use of the property may remain unchanged.
The distinction lies in how title is recorded and administered.

Role Coordination in a Real Property Context

Because real property is subject to local recording systems and jurisdiction-specific law, clarity of trustee authority and documentation precision are especially important.

The trust instrument typically defines:

- Trustee powers related to conveyance or encumbrance
- Beneficial interest structure
- Succession of trustee authority

The structure centralizes administrative control without necessarily altering day-to-day property use.

Common Asset Orientation

Land trusts generally hold:

- Residential real property
- Investment or rental property
- Undeveloped land

Asset alignment focuses specifically on title ownership rather than diversified asset administration.

Administrative Considerations

Real property held in trust may require coordination with:

- Local recording authorities
- Property tax records
- Lender or mortgage documentation
- Applicable jurisdictional statutes

Trust governance must align with property law requirements.

What This Trust Type Is Not

A land trust is not:

- A substitute for compliance with real estate law
- A universal privacy guarantee
- A mechanism that eliminates property-related obligations

It is a structural vehicle for holding and administering title.

Framework Flexibility

Land trusts may be structured within either:

- Revocable frameworks (retained authority)
- Irrevocable frameworks (separated control)

The defining feature is asset focus — not permanence.

Key Takeaway

A land trust applies traditional trust architecture to real property title.

It separates legal title from beneficial interest while centralizing administrative authority.

The trust does not change the nature of the property.
It changes how ownership is structured and documented.

BUSINESS / LLC-HOLDING TRUST

(Educational Overview)

What This Trust Type Focuses On

A Business or LLC Holding Trust is a trust structure designed to hold ownership interests in a business entity rather than directly operate the business itself.

The trust governs the ownership layer.
The entity governs operations.

This distinction is central.

Why These Trusts Are Explored

Business-holding trusts are commonly examined when:

- Ownership continuity is a priority
- Succession planning must avoid operational disruption
- Multiple beneficiaries require coordinated equity administration
- Incapacity or death planning intersects with business governance

The trust does not replace the entity's operating agreement.
It provides structured administration of ownership interests.

Structural Orientation

In a typical arrangement:

- The trust holds membership or equity interests
- The trustee administers those ownership rights pursuant to written terms
- The business continues operating under its governing documents

Operational authority remains governed by the entity's operating agreement, bylaws, or shareholder agreements.

Ownership and operation are intentionally separated.

Role Coordination in a Business Context

Because business entities operate under contractual frameworks, trustee authority must align with:

- Operating agreement provisions
- Transfer restrictions
- Consent requirements
- Voting rights and managerial structure

The trust structure must coordinate with entity governance — not override it.

Common Asset Orientation

Business-holding trusts typically hold:

- LLC membership interests
- Closely held corporate shares
- Partnership interests
- Defined equity ownership rights

The asset focus is ownership — not management.

Administrative Considerations

Trustees administering business interests may need to coordinate:

- Ownership documentation
- Voting rights
- Buy-sell agreements
- Succession triggers
- Distribution of profits or retained earnings

Clarity of authority is essential to prevent operational friction.

What This Trust Type Is Not

A business-holding trust is not:

- A substitute for an operating agreement
- A management structure for daily business operations
- A guarantee of tax classification or liability outcome

It is a governance framework for equity administration.

Framework Flexibility

Business interests may be held within:

- Revocable structures (lifetime flexibility)
- Irrevocable structures (separated ownership and long-term succession)

The choice reflects governance intent — not the nature of the business itself.

Key Takeaway

A business-holding trust separates ownership continuity from operational management.

The trust governs equity.
The entity governs operations.

Clear separation preserves both structure and stability.

INTELLECTUAL PROPERTY TRUST

(Educational Overview)

What This Trust Type Focuses On

An Intellectual Property (IP) Trust is a trust structure designed to hold and administer intangible rights rather than physical property.

These rights may include creative works, licensing agreements, patents, trademarks, or royalty interests.

The trust governs ownership and administration of the rights — not the creative process itself.

Why These Trusts Are Explored

Intellectual property often:

- Generates ongoing royalty income
- Requires contract management
- Involves licensing renewals or negotiations
- Extends beyond the creator's lifetime

Without structured oversight, administration may become fragmented or inconsistent.

A trust provides centralized governance for rights management and income continuity.

Structural Orientation

In a typical IP trust:

- The trust holds ownership interests in designated intellectual property
- The trustee administers licensing and royalty oversight pursuant to defined authority
- Income generated is managed and distributed according to written terms

The structure separates intangible rights governance from personal ownership.

Role Coordination in an Intangible Context

Because intellectual property frequently operates within contractual and statutory frameworks, trustee authority may involve:

- Overseeing licensing agreements
- Collecting and administering royalties
- Coordinating renewals within defined authority
- Preserving rights according to applicable law

The trust must align with governing intellectual property statutes and contractual obligations.

Common Asset Orientation

Intellectual property trusts may hold:

- Copyrighted works
- Patent or trademark rights
- Licensing agreements
- Royalty interests

The asset focus is intangible rights administration.

Administrative Considerations

Trustees may need to coordinate:

- Contractual renewal schedules
- Royalty accounting
- Recordkeeping for rights management
- Succession of oversight authority

Clarity of documentation is essential where income depends on ongoing licensing relationships.

What This Trust Type Is Not

An intellectual property trust is not:

- A substitute for copyright or patent registration
- A creative management entity
- A guarantee of royalty income

It is a governance framework for rights administration.

Framework Flexibility

Intellectual property may be held within:

- Revocable frameworks (lifetime coordination)
- Irrevocable frameworks (long-term rights preservation)

The architectural model reflects governance objectives — not the nature of the asset.

Key Takeaway

An intellectual property trust centralizes oversight of intangible rights.

The trust governs ownership and administration.
Creative activity and contractual execution operate within defined authority.

Structure preserves continuity where rights extend beyond individual participation.

SPECIAL NEEDS TRUST

(Educational Overview)

What This Trust Type Focuses On

A Special Needs Trust (SNT) is a trust structure designed to provide supplemental support to a beneficiary with a disability while maintaining structured oversight of distributions.

The defining feature is discretionary administration aligned with defined support standards rather than unrestricted beneficiary control.

Why These Trusts Are Explored

Special Needs Trusts are commonly examined when:

- A beneficiary relies on structured assistance
- Long-term support must be coordinated
- Oversight is necessary to manage distributions responsibly
- Continuity planning extends beyond a caregiver's lifetime

The objective is supplemental support — not replacement of existing systems.

Structural Orientation

In a typical SNT:

- The trustee holds and administers assets
- The beneficiary does not control principal
- Distributions are governed by defined standards and trustee discretion
- Administrative continuity is prioritized

The structure separates beneficial support from direct ownership.

Role Coordination in a Support Context

Because special needs planning often intersects with regulatory frameworks, trustee discretion must align with:

- Applicable public benefit systems
- Defined supplemental distribution standards
- Long-term oversight obligations

Clarity of trustee authority is essential.

Distribution language is typically structured to avoid automatic entitlement.

Common Asset Orientation

Special Needs Trusts may hold:

- Investment accounts
- Cash reserves
- Income-producing assets
- Designated family support funds

Asset alignment reflects long-term supplemental planning objectives.

Administrative Considerations

Trustees administering an SNT may need to coordinate:

- Distribution timing and purpose
- Recordkeeping and reporting
- Beneficiary care planning
- Successor trustee continuity

Administrative discipline supports stability across time.

What This Trust Type Is Not

A Special Needs Trust is not:

- A substitute for regulatory compliance
- A guarantee of benefit eligibility
- An unrestricted financial access vehicle

It is a structured governance tool designed to supplement support within defined boundaries.

Framework Flexibility

Special Needs Trusts are often structured within irrevocable frameworks, though design depends on governing objectives and applicable law.

The defining feature is discretionary support administration — not permanence alone.

Key Takeaway

A Special Needs Trust centralizes asset administration to provide structured supplemental support.

The trustee governs distributions.
The beneficiary receives benefit within defined parameters.

Structure promotes stability, continuity, and oversight.

EDUCATION TRUST

(Educational Overview)

What This Trust Type Focuses On

An Education Trust is a trust structure designed to fund educational expenses pursuant to defined standards and governance rules.

The defining feature is purpose-restricted distribution rather than general beneficiary access.

Why These Trusts Are Explored

Education trusts are commonly examined when:

- Structured funding of tuition or academic expenses is desired
- Distribution timing must align with educational milestones
- Oversight is preferred over lump-sum inheritance
- Long-term educational intent requires documented continuity

The objective is disciplined allocation tied to defined educational criteria.

Structural Orientation

In a typical education trust:

- The trustee administers assets
- Distributions are restricted to defined educational purposes
- Beneficiary access is conditioned on qualifying expenses
- Oversight extends across defined academic stages

The structure separates educational funding from unrestricted inheritance.

Role Coordination in a Purpose-Restricted Context

Because educational funding is purpose-specific, trustee authority typically includes:

- Evaluating qualifying expenses
- Coordinating payment timing
- Preserving principal where appropriate
- Maintaining documentation

Distribution standards are clearly articulated to prevent ambiguity.

Common Asset Orientation

Education trusts may hold:

- Investment accounts
- Designated savings or funding reserves
- Income-producing assets aligned with academic timelines

Asset selection reflects anticipated funding duration and distribution sequencing.

Administrative Considerations

Trustees may need to coordinate:

- Tuition payments or reimbursement procedures
- Academic verification requirements
- Distribution caps or stage-based limits
- Successor trustee continuity

Administrative clarity ensures distributions align with defined educational intent.

What This Trust Type Is Not

An education trust is not:

- An unrestricted inheritance vehicle
- A substitute for academic planning
- A guarantee of educational outcome

It is a governance structure that aligns financial resources with educational purpose.

Framework Flexibility

Education trusts may operate within revocable or irrevocable frameworks depending on broader governance objectives.

The defining characteristic is distribution restriction based on educational criteria.

Key Takeaway

An Education Trust directs resources toward defined academic purposes under fiduciary oversight.

The trustee governs eligibility.
The beneficiary receives support within structured parameters.

Purpose guides distribution.

FIREARMS TRUST

(Educational Overview)

What This Trust Type Focuses On

A Firearms Trust is a trust structure designed to hold regulated property subject to federal, state, or local legal requirements.

The defining feature is compliance-oriented governance combined with documented succession planning.

Why These Trusts Are Explored

Firearms trusts are commonly examined when:

- Regulated property requires structured oversight
- Lawful possession and succession must be documented
- Multiple authorized individuals require clarity of authority
- Continuity planning intersects with regulatory compliance

The objective is lawful administration — not operational use.

Structural Orientation

In a typical firearms trust:

- The trustee holds legal authority over regulated property
- Authorized persons are defined pursuant to governing law
- Succession of responsibility is clearly documented
- Recordkeeping is emphasized

The structure centralizes oversight within defined fiduciary boundaries.

Role Coordination in a Regulated Context

Because regulated property is governed by statutory and administrative frameworks, trustee authority must align with:

- Applicable federal and state regulations
- Transfer and possession requirements
- Documentation standards
- Succession compliance

The trust must coordinate with governing law at all times.

Common Asset Orientation

Firearms trusts may hold:

- Regulated tangible property
- Associated legal documentation
- Ownership records required for lawful administration

Asset alignment prioritizes compliance and documentation integrity.

Administrative Considerations

Trustees may need to coordinate:

- Lawful possession standards
- Documentation maintenance
- Transfer procedures consistent with governing law
- Successor trustee transition

Clarity of authority reduces risk of regulatory misalignment.

What This Trust Type Is Not

A firearms trust is not:

- A substitute for regulatory compliance
- A mechanism to bypass legal requirements
- An operational guide for property use

It is a governance structure for lawful administration and succession planning.

Framework Flexibility

Firearms trusts may operate within revocable or irrevocable frameworks depending on broader planning objectives.

The defining feature is compliance-aware administration — not structural permanence alone.

Key Takeaway

A firearms trust centralizes oversight of regulated property within a documented fiduciary framework.

Authority is defined.
Succession is structured.
Compliance governs administration.

SECTION 7 — REVOCABLE TRUST FRAMEWORK

(Architectural Analysis)

What "Revocable" Means

A revocable trust is a governance structure that retains amendment authority during the grantor's lifetime.

The defining characteristic is retained control.

The trust may generally be modified, restated, or revoked by the grantor, subject to governing law.

Core Structural Characteristics

In a typical revocable framework:

- The grantor retains amendment authority
- The grantor may serve as trustee
- Assets may be added or removed
- Successor trustees are designated for continuity

Flexibility exists within a defined fiduciary structure.

Role Consolidation and Governance

Revocable trusts often allow overlapping roles.

The grantor may simultaneously act as:

- Grantor
- Trustee
- Lifetime beneficiary

Even when roles consolidate, fiduciary standards and written terms govern administration.

Flexibility modifies authority.
It does not eliminate structure.

Administrative Orientation

Revocable trusts are frequently explored for:

- Asset organization
- Incapacity planning
- Succession coordination
- Centralized administration

They function as lifetime governance frameworks that transition upon defined triggering events.

Structural Limits

A revocable trust does not inherently:

- Eliminate tax obligations
- Provide automatic asset protection
- Replace professional drafting
- Remove fiduciary responsibility

Its primary function is organizational continuity.

Key Takeaway

A revocable trust preserves lifetime control while establishing administrative structure.

Flexibility defines the framework.
Continuity supports it.

SECTION 8 — IRREVOCABLE TRUST FRAMEWORK

(Architectural Analysis)

What "Irrevocable" Means

An irrevocable trust is a governance structure designed to operate according to predefined terms once established.

The defining characteristic is restricted modification.

Amendment authority is generally limited or unavailable, subject to applicable law.

Core Structural Characteristics

In a typical irrevocable framework:

- Roles are intentionally separated
- The grantor relinquishes defined retained powers
- Trustee authority operates independently
- Administration is structured for continuity

Permanence shapes the design.

Role Separation and Governance Discipline

Irrevocable trusts emphasize separation between:

- Grantor
- Trustee
- Beneficiaries

This separation clarifies responsibility and reinforces fiduciary accountability.

Authority is allocated deliberately rather than consolidated.

Administrative Orientation

Irrevocable trusts are commonly examined in contexts involving:

- Long-term planning
- Defined governance objectives
- Structured succession
- Multi-year or multi-generational continuity

The framework prioritizes stability over adaptability.

Structural Limits

An irrevocable trust does not inherently:

- Eliminate tax obligations
- Guarantee asset protection
- Override statutory requirements
- Remove fiduciary standards

Its distinguishing feature is structural separation and continuity.

Key Takeaway

An irrevocable trust limits modification in favor of governance discipline.

Authority is separated.
Administration is structured for endurance.

SECTION 9 — EXECUTION, FILING & ONGOING MANAGEMENT

(Structural Implementation Overview)

Why This Section Matters

Understanding trust architecture establishes structure.
Implementation determines whether that structure functions.

This section provides a high-level overview of execution, asset alignment, and ongoing administration. It offers structural orientation — not procedural instruction.

Execution: Formal Completion

Execution refers to the formal completion of the trust instrument.

This generally includes:

- Signature by the grantor
- Trustee acknowledgment where applicable
- Compliance with required formalities

Execution standards are governed by jurisdiction and trust classification.
Enforceability depends on compliance with applicable law.

Formalities & Documentation

Depending on governing law, execution may require:

- Witness signatures
- Notarization or acknowledgment
- Trustee acceptance

Not all trust structures require identical formalities.
Authority is validated through compliance with jurisdictional standards.

Filing & Public Record

Trust instruments are typically private documents.

A trust itself is not ordinarily filed with a government authority unless required by specific asset types or regulatory circumstances.

However, external documentation may reference the trust, including:

- Real property records
- Financial institution registrations
- Entity ownership records

Recording requirements depend on asset classification and jurisdiction.

Funding & Asset Alignment

A signed trust does not automatically govern assets.

For a trust to function as intended, asset ownership or designation must align with the trust structure.

This alignment may involve:

- Retitling property
- Assigning ownership interests
- Updating beneficiary designations
- Coordinating with institutional requirements

Without proper alignment, assets may remain outside trust governance.

Trustee Administration

Once operative, trustee responsibilities generally include:

- Managing trust-associated assets
- Acting pursuant to written terms
- Maintaining organized records
- Exercising fiduciary judgment

Administration reflects architecture in action.

Recordkeeping & Continuity

Clear documentation supports stability.

Effective administration typically includes:

- Financial record maintenance
- Documentation of significant decisions
- Retention of governing instruments
- Periodic structural awareness

Disciplined recordkeeping reinforces governance continuity.

Amendment & Structural Adjustment

Some trust frameworks permit amendment; others restrict modification.

Where amendment authority exists, changes must comply with governing terms and applicable formalities.

Where modification is limited, structural permanence governs.

Authority to amend is determined by the selected framework.

Periodic Review

Trust structures may warrant review when:

- Family circumstances evolve
- Asset composition changes
- Trustee roles shift
- Governing law develops

Review supports alignment.
It does not automatically require amendment.

Structural Perspective

A trust is not static.

It is a governance framework implemented through execution, alignment, and administration.

Architecture defines structure.
Implementation sustains it.

SECTION 10 — TAX & STRUCTURAL THEORY

(High-Level Governance Context)

Why Tax Is Associated with Trust Structure

Trust discussions frequently intersect with tax terminology because legal classification depends on structure.

A trust does not eliminate tax obligations.
It establishes a governance framework.

How that framework is treated for reporting or taxation purposes depends on statutory law — not the mere existence of the trust instrument.

Understanding structural distinctions clarifies why tax considerations arise in governance conversations.

Structure and Legal Classification

A trust is a legal arrangement.

Its classification depends on:

- Structural design
- Degree of retained authority
- Relationship between grantor and trustee
- Nature of trust-held assets
- Applicable governing law

The document alone does not determine treatment.
Classification results from structure applied within jurisdictional rules.

Conceptual Classification Language

In high-level discussions, trusts are described using terms such as:

- Grantor-oriented structures
- Non-grantor-oriented structures
- Pass-through treatment
- Separate entity treatment

These labels describe structural relationships.
They do not guarantee outcome.

Precise classification depends on statutory interpretation and administration.

Control and Structural Implications

A recurring theme in trust design is the relationship between:

- Retained control
- Role separation
- Legal classification

Greater retained authority may correspond with one type of treatment.
Clear separation of authority may correspond with another.

Structure influences classification — but law determines it.

Common Misconceptions

A trust does not:

- Automatically eliminate tax obligations
- Receive uniform treatment across jurisdictions
- Produce specific outcomes through template language alone

Legal treatment reflects structure, drafting precision, asset composition, and governing law.

Why Trusts Persist

Trusts endure across generations not because they remove obligations, but because they provide:

- Governance continuity
- Defined authority
- Coordinated administration
- Structured succession

Tax considerations follow structure.
They do not define it.

Asset Context

Different asset categories may interact differently with trust governance, including:

- Financial accounts
- Real property
- Business interests
- Digital assets
- Intellectual property

A trust does not alter the fundamental nature of an asset.
It establishes governance around it.

Structural Perspective

A trust is a governance framework.

Tax treatment is the application of law to structure.

Understanding this distinction prevents misplaced expectations and supports informed decision-making.

Key Takeaway

Trusts do not create tax outcomes.

They create governance architecture.

Legal classification flows from structure operating within applicable law.

Clarity precedes strategy.

Key Takeaway

SECTION 11 — CUSTOMIZATION & PROFESSIONAL REVIEW

(Responsible Use of Structural Frameworks)

Why Customization Exists

No two governance situations are identical.

Differences in:

- Family structure
- Asset composition
- Jurisdiction
- Long-term intent
- Trustee selection

Produce structural variation.

Trust frameworks are adapted — not duplicated.

Structural Foundation of This Guide

The models presented in this guide are architectural foundations.

They illustrate:

- Governance structure
- Role coordination
- Distribution philosophy
- Administrative sequencing

They are structural starting points.

Effective drafting refines architecture to reflect specific circumstances.
This guide mirrors that philosophy.

What Customization Involves

Customization may include:

- Refining role definitions
- Adjusting trustee succession language
- Clarifying distribution standards
- Aligning provisions with governing law
- Coordinating asset documentation

The degree of customization depends on objectives and jurisdictional context.

Professional Review

Trust instruments may carry long-term legal and financial implications.

Professional review is commonly sought to:

- Confirm compliance with applicable law
- Ensure internal consistency
- Address jurisdiction-specific formalities
- Coordinate asset alignment

Professional involvement strengthens enforceability and precision.
It complements structural understanding.

Deliberate Progress

Structural understanding does not require immediate execution.

There is no obligation to:

- Finalize documents
- Transfer assets
- Select a framework prematurely

Governance design benefits from clarity rather than urgency.

Structural Perspective

Trust planning is governance design.

Customization aligns structure with intention.
Professional review supports enforceability.
Implementation reflects informed architecture.

Key Takeaway

A trust framework becomes effective when structure, drafting, and implementation operate in alignment.

Understanding architecture precedes execution.
Clarity supports durable governance.

SECTION 12 — STRUCTURAL MODEL ILLUSTRATION

(Clause + Commentary Format)

Orientation

The models below demonstrate how trust architecture is expressed in formal drafting format.

They are:

- Structural illustrations
- Clause-format examples
- Not complete instruments
- Not jurisdiction-specific

Their purpose is to show how governance roles and authority are articulated within document structure.

MODEL 1 — REVOCABLE FRAMEWORK

ARTICLE I — TRUST NAME & DECLARATION

Illustrative Clause

This Trust Agreement is made on [Date], by [Grantor Name], establishing a trust known as:
[Trust Name].
This trust is intended to operate as a revocable trust subject to applicable law.

Structural Commentary

This Article establishes identity and classification.
It declares the trust relationship but does not transfer assets.

ARTICLE II — IDENTIFICATION OF PARTIES

Illustrative Clause

Grantor: [Name]
Trustee: [Name]
Successor Trustee(s): [Name(s)]

Structural Commentary

This Article defines governance roles.
Clear designation supports continuity and administrative clarity.

ARTICLE III — PURPOSE

Illustrative Clause

The purpose of this trust is to provide a structured framework for the management and administration of trust assets pursuant to its terms.

Structural Commentary

Purpose language is typically broad.
It frames intent without limiting lawful flexibility.

ARTICLE IV — REVOCABILITY

Illustrative Clause

The Grantor reserves the right to amend or revoke this trust during lifetime, subject to applicable law.

Structural Commentary

Revocability defines retained authority.
It shapes interpretation of all subsequent provisions.

ARTICLE V — FUNDING

Illustrative Clause

Property transferred to the trust shall constitute trust property.

Structural Commentary

The trust document establishes structure.
Asset control depends on proper transfer and alignment.

ARTICLE VI — TRUSTEE POWERS

Illustrative Clause

The Trustee shall administer the trust in accordance with its terms and fiduciary standards.

Structural Commentary

Authority is fiduciary, not personal ownership.
Powers are limited by document and law.

ARTICLE VII — BENEFICIARIES

Illustrative Clause

Beneficiaries shall receive distributions pursuant to the terms herein.

Structural Commentary

Beneficiary rights arise from defined standards — not automatic entitlement.

ARTICLE VIII — SUCCESSION

Illustrative Clause

A Successor Trustee shall assume authority if the acting Trustee cannot serve.

Structural Commentary

Succession provisions preserve continuity.

ARTICLE IX — ADMINISTRATION

Illustrative Clause

The trust shall be administered in good faith pursuant to its governing terms.

Structural Commentary

Administrative provisions support interpretive stability.

ARTICLE X — GOVERNING LAW

Illustrative Clause

This trust shall be governed by the laws of [Jurisdiction].

Structural Commentary

Jurisdiction anchors interpretation.

ARTICLE XI — SIGNATURES

Illustrative Clause

Executed as of the date above.
Grantor: _______
Trustee: _______

Structural Commentary

Execution formalizes the framework.

MODEL 2 — IRREVOCABLE FRAMEWORK

The structural layout mirrors the revocable model.
The distinction lies in authority allocation.

ARTICLE I — TRUST NAME & DECLARATION

Illustrative Clause

This Trust Agreement is made on [Date], by [Grantor Name], establishing a trust known as:
[Trust Name].
This trust is intended to operate as an irrevocable trust subject to applicable law.

Structural Commentary

This Article establishes identity and classification.
Irrevocability signals that the trust is designed to function independently once established.

ARTICLE II — IDENTIFICATION OF PARTIES

Illustrative Clause

Grantor: [Name]
Trustee: [Name]
Successor Trustee(s): [Name(s)]

Structural Commentary

In irrevocable structures, role separation is typically more pronounced.
Clear designation reinforces governance clarity and distinguishes authority from grantor control.

ARTICLE III — PURPOSE

Illustrative Clause

The purpose of this trust is to establish a long-term governance framework for the administration and
management of trust assets pursuant to its terms.

Structural Commentary

Purpose language in irrevocable trusts often emphasizes durability and structured independence.

ARTICLE IV — IRREVOCABILITY

Illustrative Clause

This trust is intended to be irrevocable. The Grantor does not retain the right to amend, modify, or revoke this trust except as expressly permitted by law or specific provisions of this agreement.

Structural Commentary

Irrevocability limits modification authority.
Administration operates independently of ongoing grantor control.

ARTICLE V — FUNDING

Illustrative Clause

Property transferred to the trust shall constitute trust property.
Once properly transferred, such property shall be administered exclusively under the terms of this trust.

Structural Commentary

Funding in an irrevocable framework is typically deliberate.
Because modification authority may be limited, asset alignment decisions carry long-term implications.

ARTICLE VI — TRUSTEE POWERS

Illustrative Clause

The Trustee shall administer the trust solely in accordance with its written terms and applicable law, exercising fiduciary authority independent of grantor control unless explicitly authorized herein.

Structural Commentary

Irrevocable trusts rely on trustee integrity and fiduciary standards.
Authority is exercised within defined boundaries.

ARTICLE VII — BENEFICIARIES

Illustrative Clause

Beneficiaries shall receive distributions pursuant to the terms of this agreement and the Trustee's defined authority.

Structural Commentary

Beneficiary rights are governed strictly by the instrument.
Distribution may be mandatory, discretionary, or standard-based depending on drafting.

ARTICLE VIII — SUCCESSION

Illustrative Clause

A Successor Trustee shall assume authority if the acting Trustee cannot serve, as provided in this agreement.

Structural Commentary

Long-term continuity is central to irrevocable frameworks.
Successor hierarchy reinforces structural durability.

ARTICLE IX — ADMINISTRATION

Illustrative Clause

The trust shall be administered in accordance with its stated purpose, fiduciary standards, and governing provisions.

Structural Commentary

Administrative provisions emphasize structural integrity and interpretive consistency across time.

ARTICLE X — GOVERNING LAW

Illustrative Clause

This trust shall be governed by and interpreted according to the laws of:
[Jurisdiction].

Structural Commentary

Jurisdiction anchors interpretation, administration, and enforceability.

ARTICLE XI — SIGNATURES

Illustrative Clause

Executed as of the date above.
Grantor: _______________________
Trustee: _______________________

Structural Commentary

Execution formalizes intent and establishes the operative framework.
Specific formalities depend on jurisdiction.

SECTION 13 — ILLUSTRATIVE TRUST EXAMPLES

(Fictional Structural Scenarios)

Purpose

The examples in this section demonstrate how trust architecture operates when applied to planning contexts.

They illustrate:

- Interaction between trust roles
- Differences between flexible and permanent frameworks
- How beneficiary design shapes governance
- How asset type influences structural adaptation

These scenarios emphasize architecture rather than drafting detail.

They are simplified to clarify structure.

Scope

The examples that follow are fictional.

They are not legal instruments, jurisdiction-specific templates, or executable documents.

Names, assets, and circumstances are illustrative only.

The focus is governance design — not enforceability.

Relationship to Prior Sections

The initial scenarios reflect foundational trust structures discussed in Section 5.

Later examples demonstrate how specialized asset-focused adaptations from Section 6 operate within those foundational frameworks.

Each scenario includes:

- Context
- Structural design
- Governance mechanics
- Distribution philosophy

This format reinforces applied understanding while preserving architectural clarity.

Orientation

As you review these examples, observe how variations in:

- Retained authority
- Role separation
- Asset composition
- Regulatory context
- Beneficiary sequencing

Alter governance outcomes.

Comparison sharpens structural literacy.

EXAMPLE 1 — REVOCABLE TRUST

(Fictional Structural Illustration)

Scenario Overview

Alex Rivera seeks to centralize personal asset administration while retaining full decision-making authority. The objective is continuity and organization — not asset separation or long-term permanence.

Flexibility remains essential. Alex wants a structure that adapts over time while preserving lifetime control and establishing clear succession in the event of incapacity.

To accomplish this, Alex implements a revocable trust as a foundational governance framework.

Structural Design

Trust Name:
The Alex Rivera Revocable Trust

Grantor: Alex Rivera
Trustee: Alex Rivera
Successor Trustee: Jordan Rivera

Primary Beneficiary (Lifetime): Alex Rivera
Remainder Beneficiaries: Designated family members

The defining characteristic of this structure is retained authority paired with documented succession planning.

Governance Mechanics

The grantor retains the right to amend, restate, or revoke the trust during lifetime.
Grantor and trustee roles remain unified.

Administrative continuity is achieved through a designated successor trustee who assumes authority only upon a defined triggering event. Until such an event occurs, management remains centralized.

Beneficiary designations may be modified during lifetime. The framework prioritizes flexibility over structural separation.

Asset Scope (Illustrative)

Assets associated with the trust may include:

- Personal residence
- Financial accounts
- Personal property
- Digital or access-based assets
- Other property properly aligned through funding procedures

The trust establishes governance.
Funding determines operational control.

Distribution Structure

During the grantor's lifetime, distributions are directed by the grantor acting as trustee.

Upon death or incapacity, administrative authority transitions to the successor trustee. Distribution then follows the written beneficiary designations without requiring structural redesign.

Why This Structure Works

This example demonstrates a model where:

- Authority remains centralized
- Amendment power is preserved
- Succession is predefined
- Governance adapts without loss of control

The emphasis is organizational clarity — not permanence.

EXAMPLE 2 — IRREVOCABLE TRUST

(Fictional Structural Illustration)

Scenario Overview

Morgan Ellis seeks to establish a governance structure designed for long-term administration under independent oversight.

Flexibility is not the objective. Durability is.

Morgan intends to separate management authority from personal ownership, restrict unilateral modification, and define distribution standards in advance. The design anticipates continuity beyond individual control.

To accomplish this, Morgan establishes an irrevocable trust.

Structural Design

Trust Name:
The Ellis Family Irrevocable Trust

Grantor: Morgan Ellis
Trustee: Independent Trustee
Successor Trustee: Designated individual or institutional fiduciary
Beneficiaries: Named individuals or entities

The defining characteristic of this structure is intentional separation between grantor and trustee.

Governance Mechanics

Once established, the trust operates pursuant to its written terms.

The grantor does not retain management authority over trust assets. Administration is conducted independently by the trustee under fiduciary standards.

Amendment authority is limited or restricted, subject to governing law and the trust instrument. Distribution decisions occur according to predefined standards rather than grantor direction.

Successor trusteeship is clearly articulated to preserve structural continuity across time.

The framework emphasizes independence, role discipline, and governance stability.

Asset Scope (Illustrative)

Assets aligned with this structure may include:

- Long-term investment portfolios
- Income-producing property
- Business interests
- Structured financial assets
- Property transferred with permanence intent

Asset alignment is approached deliberately due to the limited modification framework. The design anticipates continuity rather than adjustment.

Distribution Structure

Distributions occur according to standards articulated in the governing instrument.

The trustee evaluates beneficiary circumstances, applies defined criteria, and exercises discretion within structured limits.

Ongoing distribution authority does not remain with the grantor once the structure is operational.

Why This Structure Works

This model demonstrates:

- Separation of authority
- Restricted amendment power
- Independent fiduciary administration
- Governance durability

Control is shifted from the individual to the framework itself.

The architecture prioritizes permanence over adaptability.

EXAMPLE 3 — FAMILY TRUST

(Fictional Structural Illustration)

Scenario Overview

Taylor Bennett seeks to establish a governance structure designed to coordinate family assets across generations.

The objective extends beyond asset transfer. It is structured stewardship — balancing support, preservation, and continuity within a unified framework.

Taylor wishes to avoid lump-sum inheritance distribution, provide support appropriate to varying life stages, and maintain long-term alignment beyond a single lifetime.

To accomplish this, Taylor establishes a family trust designed for intergenerational governance.

Structural Design

Trust Name:
The Bennett Family Trust

Grantor: Taylor Bennett
Trustee: Independent Trustee
Successor Trustee: Designated individual or institutional fiduciary
Beneficiaries: Children and future descendants

This structure is beneficiary-centered rather than grantor-centered.

Depending on design intent, it may operate as revocable during lifetime or irrevocable to reinforce permanence. The defining characteristic is not classification — but coordination among multiple beneficiaries.

Governance Mechanics

The trustee administers assets for the benefit of multiple beneficiaries simultaneously.

Distribution authority is guided by defined standards and fiduciary discretion. Principal preservation is balanced against present support needs, with attention to generational sustainability.

Succession planning is embedded within the framework to ensure continuity beyond the original grantor.

The model emphasizes discretion, balance, and long-term alignment rather than automatic entitlement.

Distribution Structure

Distributions may be guided by structured standards such as:

- Health
- Education
- Maintenance
- Support

The trustee evaluates beneficiary circumstances within the broader context of trust sustainability and generational equity.

Assets are not automatically distributed at a single age milestone unless expressly defined. Instead, distribution philosophy reinforces stewardship over immediate ownership.

Asset Scope (Illustrative)

Assets aligned with this structure may include:

- Real property intended for shared or generational benefit
- Long-term investment portfolios
- Business interests
- Income-producing property
- Financial accounts designated for structured distribution

Asset selection reflects preservation, coordination, and continuity objectives.

Why This Structure Works

This model demonstrates governance layered across beneficiaries rather than concentrated in a single authority holder.

Its architectural focus is intergenerational continuity — balancing present access with long-term preservation through fiduciary discretion.

EXAMPLE 4 — MARITAL / QTIP TRUST

(Fictional Structural Illustration)

Scenario Overview

Jordan Patel seeks to provide lifetime financial security for a surviving spouse while preserving defined assets for children from a prior relationship.

The objective is structured sequencing — ensuring present support without surrendering ultimate distribution intent.

Jordan wishes to provide stable income to the spouse, preserve principal for remainder beneficiaries, and prevent unintended redirection of long-term assets. The structure must maintain fiduciary neutrality between present and future interests.

To accomplish this, Jordan establishes a marital trust incorporating QTIP-style provisions.

Structural Design

Trust Name:
The Patel Marital Trust

Grantor: Jordan Patel
Trustee: Independent Trustee

Primary Beneficiary (Lifetime): Surviving Spouse
Remainder Beneficiaries: Designated children from prior relationship

The defining structural characteristic is the separation between lifetime beneficial enjoyment and ultimate ownership.

Governance Mechanics

During the spouse's lifetime, income generated by trust assets may be distributed according to defined standards. Principal distributions may be limited or subject to trustee discretion, depending on the governing terms.

The trustee must balance income obligations with preservation of corpus. Beneficial enjoyment does not include authority to redirect remainder interests.

Upon the spouse's death, remaining principal passes to the designated remainder beneficiaries in accordance with the written sequencing of the trust instrument.

Ownership does not merge during the spouse's lifetime. The trustee administers the structure under fiduciary standards that recognize competing present and future interests.

Distribution Structure

This framework distinguishes clearly between:

- Income rights (lifetime benefit)
- Principal rights (future remainder interest)

The surviving spouse may receive required income distributions and discretionary support within defined parameters. However, preservation of principal remains central to long-term intent.

The architecture prevents unilateral reallocation of remainder assets.

Asset Scope (Illustrative)

Assets aligned with this structure may include:

- Income-producing investment portfolios
- Dividend or interest-bearing accounts
- Rental real estate
- Closely held business interests
- Long-term preservation assets

Asset selection typically reflects the need to balance income generation with principal stability.

Why This Structure Works

This model formalizes ordered succession of benefit.

It separates lifetime support from ultimate ownership, preserves remainder intent, and reinforces fiduciary neutrality across competing interests.

The architectural focus is controlled succession rather than joint ownership.

EXAMPLE 5 — SPENDTHRIFT TRUST

(Fictional Structural Illustration)

Scenario Overview

Olivia Grant seeks to provide long-term financial support for a beneficiary who has demonstrated difficulty managing unrestricted access to funds.

The objective is protection and sustainability — ensuring that assets remain available over time rather than subject to premature depletion or external pressure.

To accomplish this, Olivia establishes a spendthrift trust incorporating defined distribution safeguards.

Structural Design

Trust Name:
The Grant Protective Trust

Grantor: Olivia Grant
Trustee: Designated Trustee
Beneficiary: Named individual

The defining structural characteristic is separation between beneficial enjoyment and asset control.

Governance Mechanics

Legal authority over trust assets remains exclusively with the trustee.

The beneficiary does not possess unilateral access to principal and may not voluntarily transfer, assign, or pledge their interest in the trust. Distribution timing and amount are determined by trustee discretion within defined standards.

Requests for distribution are evaluated in light of long-term preservation objectives rather than automatic entitlement. The trustee's role is protective as well as administrative.

This framework centralizes authority under fiduciary oversight to maintain sustainability.

Distribution Structure

Distributions occur according to:

- Defined discretionary standards
- Evaluation of beneficiary need
- Preservation of principal

The beneficiary's interest is limited to distributions authorized under the governing instrument. Direct control over corpus and assignment of beneficial interest are restricted by design.

The architecture prioritizes controlled access over ownership transfer.

Asset Scope (Illustrative)

Assets aligned with this structure may include:

- Investment portfolios
- Cash reserves
- Income-producing assets
- Structured financial accounts

Asset selection typically reflects the need for measured distribution and administrative discipline.

Why This Structure Works

This model reinforces protection through structural restraint.

By separating access from authority, it preserves resources for sustained benefit while maintaining fiduciary oversight.

The architectural emphasis is containment, discipline, and continuity.

EXAMPLE 6 — CHARITABLE TRUST

(Fictional Structural Illustration)

Scenario Overview

Daniel Harper seeks to formalize long-term philanthropic intent within a structured governance framework.

The objective is mission continuity — ensuring that charitable support occurs deliberately and consistently rather than through episodic decision-making.

To accomplish this, Daniel establishes a charitable trust dedicated exclusively to a defined charitable purpose.

Structural Design

Trust Name:
The Harper Charitable Trust

Grantor: Daniel Harper
Trustee: Independent Trustee
Charitable Beneficiary: Designated organization or stated charitable purpose

The defining characteristic of this structure is purpose-based governance rather than personal or family benefit.

Governance Mechanics

Trust assets are dedicated solely to charitable objectives.

Distributions occur according to predefined standards, which may include timing schedules, percentage allocations, or structured sequencing. The trustee administers assets under fiduciary standards aligned with mission preservation.

Personal or family benefit is excluded from the framework. Administrative decisions must remain consistent with the trust's stated purpose.

The architecture aligns fiduciary authority with sustained public or philanthropic objectives.

Distribution Structure

All distributions are guided by mission rather than entitlement.

The trustee ensures that:

- Funds are applied in alignment with the stated charitable objective
- Administrative discipline supports long-term sustainability
- Asset management reinforces continuity of purpose

The structure prioritizes mission stability over flexibility of redirection.

Asset Scope (Illustrative)

Assets aligned with this structure may include:

- Investment portfolios designated for charitable distribution
- Appreciated financial assets
- Income-generating property
- Endowment-style holdings

Asset selection typically reflects sustainability and structured distribution objectives.

Why This Structure Works

This model formalizes philanthropic intent within a durable governance framework.

By separating charitable purpose from personal interest, it preserves mission integrity through fiduciary oversight and structured administration.

The architectural emphasis is alignment, sustainability, and continuity of purpose.

EXAMPLE 7 — LAND TRUST

(Fictional Structural Illustration)

Scenario Overview

Samantha Cole owns real property and seeks to structure title ownership in a manner that separates record title from beneficial interest.

The objective is administrative clarity — centralizing property governance while distinguishing between legal title and beneficial control.

To accomplish this, Samantha establishes a land trust.

Structural Design

Trust Name:
The Cole Property Land Trust

Grantor: Samantha Cole
Trustee: Designated Title Trustee
Beneficial Interest Holder(s): Samantha Cole (initially), with transferable beneficial interest provisions

The defining structural characteristic is separation between legal title and beneficial ownership.

Governance Mechanics

Legal title to the property is held by the trustee. Beneficial interest remains separate from record ownership.

The trustee's authority is typically administrative and title-focused, rather than discretionary in the traditional distribution sense. Beneficial interest may be transferred without altering recorded title, depending on governing terms.

This framework can simplify succession planning, fractional ownership adjustments, and continuity of title without repeated public re-recording.

The architecture distinguishes clearly between title control and beneficial control.

Distribution Structure

Land trusts do not generally emphasize periodic distributions in the traditional support-oriented sense.

Governance centers on:

- Control of beneficial interest
- Income or use rights associated with the property
- Transfer of beneficial interest according to defined provisions

Distributions, where applicable, typically relate to rental income or sale proceeds rather than structured support payments.

The framework emphasizes title mechanics over beneficiary layering.

Asset Scope (Illustrative)

Assets aligned with this structure are typically:

- Real property
- Income-producing real estate
- Undeveloped land
- Property held for investment or structured ownership

The land trust is asset-specific by design.

Why This Structure Works

This model formalizes separation between public record ownership and beneficial interest.

By centralizing title while preserving transferable beneficial rights, it supports administrative continuity and structured property governance.

The architectural emphasis is title clarity and ownership structuring.

EXAMPLE 8 — BUSINESS-HOLDING TRUST

(Fictional Structural Illustration)

Scenario Overview

Marcus Lee owns a closely held LLC and seeks to establish structured ownership continuity without disrupting operational management.

The objective is succession stability — preserving entity operations while formalizing transfer of equity interests.

To accomplish this, Marcus establishes a trust to hold the LLC membership interests.

Structural Design

Trust Name:
The Lee Ownership Trust

Grantor: Marcus Lee
Trustee: Designated Trustee
Asset Held: 100% LLC Membership Interest

The defining structural characteristic is separation between ownership governance and entity operations.

Governance Mechanics

The trust holds legal ownership of the LLC membership interest. The trustee administers ownership rights in accordance with the trust's governing terms.

Operational authority remains governed by the LLC's operating agreement. The business continues functioning as a separate legal entity.

Trustee authority relates to ownership rights — voting, transfer, and succession — rather than day-to-day operational control unless expressly provided.

The architecture creates layered governance:

- Trust → Ownership Layer
- LLC → Operational Layer

Succession of equity interests occurs within the trust framework without requiring structural redesign of the business entity itself.

Distribution Structure

Distributions may occur at two levels:

Entity Level:
 The LLC may generate profits or make distributions pursuant to its operating agreement.

Trust Level:
 Distributions received by the trust are administered according to the trust's governing provisions.

The trust governs beneficial enjoyment of equity interests, not operational execution of business activity.

The structure prioritizes orderly ownership transition while preserving operational continuity.

Asset Scope (Illustrative)

Assets aligned with this structure may include:

- LLC membership interests
- Shares in closely held corporations
- Partnership interests
- Equity subject to operating agreements

Asset alignment centers on ownership administration rather than direct business management.

Why This Structure Works

This model integrates entity governance with trust-based ownership administration.

By separating operational authority from equity succession, it preserves contractual continuity, vendor relationships, and business stability while formalizing long-term ownership transition.

The architectural emphasis is layered governance and structural continuity.

EXAMPLE 9 — INTELLECTUAL PROPERTY TRUST

(Fictional Structural Illustration)

Scenario Overview

Ava Reynolds is an author with an active portfolio of copyrighted works, licensing agreements, and ongoing royalty streams.

The objective is continuity of rights administration — ensuring that creative assets remain governed, licensed, and monetized beyond personal involvement.

To accomplish this, Ava transfers designated intellectual property interests into a trust.

Structural Design

Trust Name:
The Reynolds Literary Trust

Grantor: Ava Reynolds
Trustee: Designated Trustee
Assets Held: Copyrighted works, licensing agreements, royalty interests

The defining structural characteristic is centralized governance of intangible rights under fiduciary administration.

Governance Mechanics

Legal ownership of specified intellectual property rights is held by the trust.

The trustee administers licensing agreements within defined authority, oversees royalty collection, and maintains contractual continuity consistent with the governing instrument. Renewals, negotiations, or enforcement actions may occur within structured limits.

The governance framework separates creative authorship from administrative oversight.

The architecture emphasizes preservation of rights and disciplined management of revenue streams.

Distribution Structure

Royalty income generated by the intellectual property:

- Is received by the trust
- Is administered pursuant to defined distribution standards
- May be retained, reinvested, or distributed according to governing provisions

The structure formalizes revenue flow rather than relying on informal collection. Distribution emphasizes continuity of rights-based income across time.

Asset Scope (Illustrative)

Assets aligned with this structure may include:

- Copyrighted literary works
- Licensing agreements
- Royalty contracts
- Trademark rights
- Patent interests
- Digital publishing rights

The trust governs intangible rights rather than physical property or operational entities.

Why This Structure Works

This model centralizes administration of intellectual rights within a durable governance framework.

By separating asset ownership from personal oversight, it preserves licensing integrity, revenue continuity, and contractual discipline.

The architectural emphasis is rights preservation and structured revenue governance.

EXAMPLE 10 — SPECIAL NEEDS TRUST

(Fictional Structural Illustration)

Scenario Overview

Elena Martinez seeks to provide long-term financial support for a beneficiary with ongoing medical and support needs.

The objective is supplemental stability — ensuring structured assistance while preserving access to essential public or institutional support programs where applicable.

To accomplish this, Elena establishes a Special Needs Trust designed to provide supplemental benefit without transferring unrestricted ownership.

Structural Design

Trust Name:
The Martinez Supplemental Support Trust

Grantor: Elena Martinez
Trustee: Designated Independent Trustee
Beneficiary: Named individual with defined support needs

The defining structural characteristic is discretionary, supplemental distribution authority.

Governance Mechanics

Legal ownership of trust assets is held by the trustee.

The beneficiary does not possess unilateral access to principal. Distributions are discretionary and structured to supplement — not replace — other available support.

The trustee evaluates requests within defined standards and in consideration of long-term stability. Mandatory or automatic distributions are typically avoided to preserve structural flexibility and eligibility alignment.

The architecture emphasizes controlled assistance rather than direct ownership.

Distribution Structure

Distributions may be made for needs such as:

- Medical or therapeutic support
- Educational assistance
- Quality-of-life enhancements
- Supplemental living expenses

The trustee retains discretion over timing, amount, and appropriateness of each distribution.

The structure is intentionally designed to avoid automatic income or principal payments that could interfere with applicable eligibility frameworks.

The emphasis remains supplemental support within structured boundaries.

Asset Scope (Illustrative)

Assets aligned with this structure may include:

- Investment portfolios
- Cash reserves
- Income-producing assets
- Long-term preservation funds

Asset alignment reflects durability and measured distribution over time.

Why This Structure Works

This model provides structured support while preserving beneficiary stability.

By separating ownership from access and embedding discretionary oversight, it reinforces continuity of care within a disciplined governance framework.

The architectural emphasis is supplemental assistance aligned with long-term well-being.

Asset Scope (Illustrative)

Assets aligned with this structure may include:

- Investment portfolios
- Cash reserves
- Income-producing assets
- Long-term preservation funds

Asset alignment reflects durability and measured distribution over time.

Structural Observations

This example illustrates:

- Discretion-based distribution authority
- Supplemental (not replacement) support philosophy
- Restriction of beneficiary control over principal
- Eligibility-sensitive governance design
- Long-term fiduciary oversight

Unlike Example 5 (Spendthrift Trust), which focuses on protecting assets from beneficiary misuse or creditor exposure, this structure focuses on preserving beneficiary support frameworks.

Unlike Example 3 (Family Trust), which coordinates multiple beneficiaries across generations, this structure centers on tailored support for a specific beneficiary.

The architectural focus is discretionary supplementation aligned with beneficiary stability.

EXAMPLE 11 — EDUCATION TRUST

(Fictional Structural Illustration)

Scenario Overview

Samuel Carter seeks to establish a structured funding mechanism dedicated exclusively to supporting future educational pursuits of designated beneficiaries.

The objective is purpose-restricted allocation — reserving assets specifically for academic advancement rather than general inheritance.

To accomplish this, Samuel establishes an Education Trust designed to provide conditional educational funding under defined standards.

Structural Design

Trust Name:
The Carter Education Trust

Grantor: Samuel Carter
Trustee: Designated Trustee
Beneficiaries: Named children or future descendants

The defining structural characteristic is purpose-restricted distribution authority.

Governance Mechanics

Legal ownership of trust assets is held by the trustee.

Distributions are limited to education-related purposes as defined in the governing instrument. The trustee verifies qualifying expenses before authorizing payment.

Funds are not automatically distributed at a single age milestone unless expressly structured. Unused funds may remain subject to continued educational qualification or alternative provisions as articulated in the trust.

The architecture centers on conditional funding rather than general discretionary support.

Distribution Structure

Distributions may be authorized for:

- Tuition and academic fees
- Required textbooks and materials
- Housing and educational living expenses
- Vocational or specialized training programs
- Other defined educational costs

The trustee evaluates eligibility, timing, and amount within the boundaries of clearly defined criteria.

The structure restricts diversion of funds to non-educational uses unless explicitly permitted.

The emphasis is targeted allocation aligned with defined academic objectives.

Asset Scope (Illustrative)

Assets aligned with this structure may include:

- Investment accounts designated for educational growth
- Structured savings portfolios
- Income-producing assets dedicated to academic funding
- Long-term educational reserve funds

Asset selection typically reflects anticipated timing of academic milestones and phased distribution needs.

Why This Structure Works

This model formalizes education funding within a criteria-based governance framework.

By conditioning access on defined academic objectives, it reinforces intentional advancement rather than unrestricted inheritance.

The architectural emphasis is milestone alignment and disciplined allocation.

EXAMPLE 12 — FIREARMS TRUST

(Fictional Structural Illustration)

Scenario Overview

Ethan Brooks seeks to establish structured oversight of regulated property subject to defined legal requirements.

The objective is continuity of lawful administration — ensuring that possession, oversight, and succession occur within established regulatory boundaries.

To accomplish this, Ethan establishes a firearms trust designed around compliance-aware governance.

Structural Design

Trust Name:
The Brooks Compliance Trust

Grantor: Ethan Brooks
Trustee: Designated Trustee
Assets Held: Regulated tangible property subject to applicable law

The defining structural characteristic is regulation-centered administration under fiduciary authority.

Governance Mechanics

Legal ownership of the regulated property is held by the trust.

Trustee authority is exercised strictly within applicable legal parameters. Authorized persons may be identified in accordance with governing law and documented appropriately.

Succession of trustee responsibility is clearly articulated to preserve continuity of lawful oversight. Recordkeeping and documentation integrity are central to administration.

Transfers, where permitted, occur only in accordance with regulatory standards and documented procedures.

The architecture prioritizes disciplined oversight and procedural continuity.

Distribution Structure

Transfer or distribution of regulated property:

- Occurs only within the constraints of applicable law
- Follows structured documentation requirements
- Remains subject to eligibility standards

The framework emphasizes lawful succession rather than discretionary allocation.

Asset Scope (Illustrative)

Assets aligned with this structure may include:

- Tangible property subject to federal, state, or local regulation
- Associated compliance documentation
- Lawfully administered property requiring structured oversight

The governance focus is regulatory integrity rather than general estate distribution.

Why This Structure Works

This model formalizes oversight of regulated assets within a documented fiduciary framework.

By centralizing lawful authority and succession procedures, it reinforces compliance continuity and administrative clarity across time.

The architectural emphasis is structured responsibility within regulatory boundaries.

EXAMPLE 13 — DIGITAL ASSET TRUST

(Fictional Structural Illustration)

Scenario Overview

Noah Bennett holds a portfolio of digital assets that rely on credential-based authorization and platform-level control rather than physical possession.

The objective is continuity of administrative authority — ensuring that digital assets remain governable beyond personal knowledge or singular access credentials.

To accomplish this, Noah establishes a Digital Asset Trust designed to align fiduciary governance with access-dependent assets.

Structural Design

Trust Name:
The Bennett Digital Asset Trust

Grantor: Noah Bennett
Trustee: Designated Trustee with defined administrative authority
Assets Held: Digital or virtual assets subject to platform-based control

The defining structural characteristic is coordination between legal ownership and system-based access control.

Governance Mechanics

Legal ownership of designated digital assets is associated with the trust.

Trustee authority is defined in accordance with the governing instrument. Administrative continuity is structured to prevent loss of governance due to incapacity or death.

Credential management and technical protocols are maintained separately from the trust document itself. The trust governs authority; external systems govern operational access.

Succession provisions ensure that fiduciary oversight transitions without disruption.

The architecture emphasizes alignment between legal authority and platform-level administration.

Distribution Structure

Digital assets may represent:

- Financial value
- Utility or access rights
- Tokenized or contractual benefits

Where distributions are applicable, they occur pursuant to the trust's governing terms.

However, the framework prioritizes continuity of authority and structured succession over automatic liquidation or informal transfer.

Asset Scope (Illustrative)

Assets aligned with this structure may include:

- Cryptographic tokens
- Digital currencies
- Blockchain-based assets
- Digital property rights
- Platform-based accounts
- Access-dependent intangible holdings

The trust governs ownership authority. Technical custody remains subject to external systems and protocols.

Why This Structure Works

This model applies traditional fiduciary architecture to assets dependent on digital access systems.

By separating legal governance from technical custody, it reinforces continuity of authority while respecting platform-based operational realities.

The architectural emphasis is structured authority alignment within evolving digital environments.

Closing Note on Illustrations

The examples in this section are presented to clarify structure through application. They translate architectural concepts into contextual form.

They are not drafting instruments, procedural guides, or jurisdiction-specific documents.

Trust implementation involves execution formalities, asset alignment, and legal compliance that depend on governing law and professional evaluation.

These illustrations exist to strengthen structural literacy.

Architecture precedes execution.

SECTION 14 — ASSETS & ANCILLARY DOCUMENTS

(Structural Relationship Overview)

Why This Section Matters

A trust agreement defines governance — roles, authority, and distribution standards.

Assets define what is governed.

Understanding the distinction between structure and property is essential to understanding how trusts function in practice.

This section provides a conceptual overview of that relationship.

Structure and Property

At a foundational level:

- The trust instrument establishes authority.
- The assets determine scope.

The existence of a trust does not, by itself, alter the legal character of property. Separate documentation typically reflects how specific assets are associated with the trust.

Clarity on this distinction prevents common misunderstandings about how governance operates.

Common Asset Categories

Trust discussions frequently involve assets such as:

- Real property
- Personal property
- Financial accounts
- Business interests
- Digital or virtual assets

Each category may operate under its own legal framework, institutional policy, or regulatory structure independent of the trust agreement.

The trust governs authority. The asset's classification governs procedure.

Ancillary Documents

In planning discussions, "ancillary documents" refer to records that exist outside the trust agreement but relate to assets governed by it.

Examples may include:

- Title or ownership records
- Institutional account agreements
- Registration documentation
- Operating agreements
- Insurance beneficiary designations

These documents are governed by applicable law and institutional standards. They operate alongside — not within — the trust instrument.

Asset Alignment vs. Asset Control

A critical distinction exists between the creation of a trust and the formal association of assets with it.

The trust establishes governance authority.
Asset alignment reflects how property is documented under that authority.

Institutions and jurisdictions may impose independent documentation or recognition requirements.

Governance design and asset documentation are related — but not interchangeable.

Administrative Perspective

From an administrative standpoint, clarity regarding asset alignment supports:

- Continuity planning
- Trustee orientation
- Record consistency
- Professional review
- Governance transparency

The trust provides structure.
Associated records reflect implementation.

Closing Perspective

Trust governance does not operate in isolation.

It functions in coordination with property records, institutional systems, and applicable law.

Understanding this coordination reinforces structural literacy and supports informed professional dialogue.

APPENDIX A — MASTER ASSET INVENTORY FRAMEWORK

(Governance Reference & Structural Alignment Tool)

Purpose

This Appendix provides a structured reference framework for identifying and organizing asset categories commonly associated with trust governance.

Its function is administrative clarity — not valuation, transfer instruction, or access documentation.

A consolidated inventory may support:

- Governance continuity
- Trustee orientation
- Professional review preparation
- Structural tier comparison
- Asset-alignment awareness

Completion of this framework is optional.
It serves as a governance reference tool — not a legal requirement.

Structural Perspective

A trust defines authority.
An asset inventory clarifies scope.

Structure without visibility creates blind spots.
Visibility without structure creates fragmentation.

This Appendix supports alignment between governance architecture and asset reality.

Sensitive credentials, passwords, or security information should not be recorded in this document.

SECTION I — TRADITIONAL FINANCIAL ASSETS

(Repeat as necessary)

Asset Description:
Asset Type:

- Checking / Savings Account
- Brokerage Account
- Retirement Account
- Certificate of Deposit
- Cash Equivalent
- Other Financial Asset

Institution / Custodian (High-Level Only):
Ownership Structure:

- Individually Owned
- Joint Ownership
- Trust-Titled
- Beneficiary Designation
- Other

Associated Trust (If Applicable):
Last Reviewed (Date):

SECTION II — REAL PROPERTY

(Repeat as necessary)

Property Description:
Property Type:

- Primary Residence
- Rental Property
- Commercial Property
- Land / Undeveloped Property
- Other Real Estate

Title Status (High-Level Only):

- Individually Held
- Joint Tenancy
- Trust-Titled
- LLC-Owned
- Other

Associated Trust (If Applicable):
Notes (High-Level Governance Context Only):
Last Reviewed (Date):

SECTION III — BUSINESS INTERESTS

(Repeat as necessary)

Business Name:
Entity Type:

- LLC
- Corporation
- Partnership
- Sole Proprietorship
- Other

Ownership Percentage:
Held By:

- Individual
- Trust
- Holding Entity
- Other

Operating Agreement Coordinated With Trust Structure?

- Yes
- No
- Not Applicable

Last Reviewed (Date):

SECTION IV — DIGITAL & VIRTUAL ASSETS

(Repeat as necessary)

Asset Description / Platform:
 Asset Category:

- Digital Currency
- Tokenized Asset
- Utility / Governance Token
- Online Revenue Source
- Domain / Intellectual Property
- Other Digital Asset

Custody Type (High-Level Only):

- Self-Custodied
- Exchange / Platform
- Third-Party Custodian
- Multi-Signature
- Other

Associated Trust (If Applicable):
 Last Reviewed (Date):

Administrative Reminder

This Appendix does not:

- Transfer ownership
- Create beneficiary designations
- Replace institutional documentation
- Establish legal title

Asset alignment must comply with applicable law and institutional requirements.

Why This Appendix Matters

Trust governance operates where structure and assets intersect.

An organized inventory may:

- Reduce oversight gaps
- Support trustee onboarding
- Clarify funding alignment
- Strengthen administrative resilience
- Improve professional coordination

Architecture without visibility creates blind spots.
Visibility without structure creates fragmentation.

This Appendix exists to support coherence between the two.

APPENDIX B — TRUSTEE ROLE BREAKDOWN

(Integrated Structural Reference)

Purpose

This Appendix provides a consolidated overview of trustee authority, governance structure, and distribution philosophy within trust design.

Trust architecture is not defined solely by asset placement.
It is defined by how authority is assigned, exercised, transitioned, and constrained across time.

This section supports structural literacy by clarifying:

- Trustee authority
- Role distribution models
- Successor hierarchy
- Discretion frameworks
- Distribution architecture principles

This Appendix is educational in nature and does not establish enforceable authority.

PART I — TRUSTEE AUTHORITY & FIDUCIARY STRUCTURE

Core Trustee Responsibilities (High-Level)

In general terms, a trustee is responsible for:

- Administering trust assets
- Following the written terms of the trust
- Acting in a fiduciary capacity
- Maintaining organized records
- Exercising discretion where permitted
- Balancing beneficiary interests when required

A trustee manages trust property but does not own it for personal benefit.

Authority exists within defined boundaries.

Fiduciary Orientation

Trustees are typically expected to act:

- In good faith
- With reasonable care
- With impartiality among beneficiaries (where applicable)
- Within the authority granted by the governing instrument

Interpretation of fiduciary obligations depends on jurisdiction and drafting precision.

Fiduciary duty is not abstract — it defines the standard by which authority is exercised.

PART II — GOVERNANCE STRUCTURE MODELS

Trust structures vary in how authority is distributed.

Model A — Unified Role Structure

(Common in Revocable Frameworks)

- Grantor and Trustee may be the same individual
- Control is largely retained
- Role separation is minimal by design

This model emphasizes flexibility and centralized authority.

Model B — Independent Trustee Structure

(Common in Irrevocable Frameworks)

- Grantor and Trustee are intentionally separated
- Administrative authority operates independently
- Governance discipline is emphasized

This model prioritizes structural durability and role distinction.

Model C — Layered Governance Structure

- Initial Trustee
- Successor Trustee
- Co-Trustee (optional)
- Trust Protector (conceptual reference only)

Layered structures may enhance administrative resilience and long-term continuity.

Authority is distributed rather than concentrated.

PART III — SUCCESSOR & CONTINUITY DESIGN

Clear succession language supports governance stability.

A simplified hierarchy may resemble:

Primary Trustee
↓
First Successor Trustee
↓
Secondary Successor Trustee
↓
Institutional Trustee (optional)

Considerations often include:

- Administrative capability
- Neutrality
- Longevity
- Financial literacy
- Geographic practicality

No universal hierarchy exists.
Continuity design reflects governance priorities.

PART IV — DISTRIBUTION ARCHITECTURE

Distribution structure often defines the practical impact of a trust.

Trustee authority may range from narrow to broad.

Mandatory Distribution Model

Distributions occur upon defined triggering events.
Emphasis: Predictability and limited discretion.

Discretionary Model

Trustee evaluates beneficiary circumstances within defined boundaries.
Emphasis: Flexibility and fiduciary judgment.

Standard-Based Model

Distributions are guided by structured standards such as:

- Health
- Education
- Maintenance
- Support

Emphasis: Structured flexibility.

Hybrid Model

Combines mandatory triggers with discretionary evaluation.
Emphasis: Layered governance across time.

Distribution architecture is where theory becomes practical effect.

PART V — REMOVAL & REPLACEMENT MECHANISMS

Some trust structures contemplate mechanisms for:

- Trustee resignation
- Beneficiary removal authority
- Court intervention
- Automatic succession
- Appointment of replacement trustees

Availability and enforceability depend on jurisdiction and governing language.

Removal provisions are structural safeguards, not default assumptions.

PART VI — GOVERNANCE REFERENCE WORKSHEET

(Structural Awareness Only)

Current Trustee:

Is the Trustee also the Grantor?

- Yes
- No

Successor Trustee(s):

Is the Trustee Independent?

- Family Member
- Professional
- Institutional
- Other

Intended Discretion Model:

- Mandatory
- Discretionary
- Standard-Based
- Hybrid

Removal Mechanism Contemplated:

- Automatic Succession
- Named Replacement
- Court-Based
- Not Addressed

High-Level Governance Notes:

Administrative Reminder

Trustee authority, discretion, and removal rights are governed by written trust language and applicable law.

This Appendix supports governance awareness — not implementation.

Why This Appendix Matters

Trust design is governance design.

Clear role definition and distribution architecture may:

- Reduce administrative ambiguity
- Support succession continuity
- Clarify fiduciary boundaries
- Strengthen structural durability

A well-structured trust reflects intentional authority architecture.

APPENDIX C — EXECUTION & FORMALITIES OVERVIEW

(Implementation Awareness — Governance Context)

Purpose

Trust governance depends on both design and implementation.

This Appendix provides a high-level overview of execution and asset-alignment considerations commonly associated with trust administration.

It is presented for awareness only.
Execution requirements are governed by jurisdiction, asset classification, and applicable law.

PART I — EXECUTION CONSIDERATIONS

Execution refers to the formal completion of a trust instrument.

It commonly includes:

- Grantor signature
- Trustee acknowledgment or acceptance (where applicable)
- Dating of the instrument
- Formal declaration language

Depending on governing law and trust classification, additional formalities may apply.

Enforceability depends on compliance with applicable standards.

This Appendix does not prescribe execution requirements.

PART II — WITNESSES & NOTARIZATION

Certain jurisdictions may require or recognize:

- Witness signatures
- Notarization
- Acknowledgment before an authorized official

Formal standards vary by jurisdiction and trust type.
Validity is determined by governing law.

PART III — FUNDING ALIGNMENT

A signed trust document does not automatically transfer asset control.

"Funding" refers to alignment between the trust instrument and asset ownership or designation.

Alignment may involve:

- Retitling property
- Assigning ownership interests
- Updating beneficiary designations
- Executing separate transfer documentation

Procedures differ by asset category and institutional policy.

Without alignment, governance authority may exist in theory but not in practice.

PART IV — REAL PROPERTY COORDINATION

(Conceptual Overview)

When real property is associated with a trust, implementation may involve:

- Deed preparation
- Recording with appropriate local authorities
- Compliance with property law formalities

Failure to properly align title documentation may limit administrative authority.

Recording standards and deed requirements are jurisdiction-specific.

PART V — BUSINESS & ENTITY COORDINATION

Where trusts hold business interests:

- Operating agreements may require review
- Transfer restrictions may apply
- Consent provisions may be implicated

Coordination between trust language and entity governing documents preserves continuity.

Misalignment can create administrative friction.

PART VI — DIGITAL & INTANGIBLE ASSET ALIGNMENT

Digital assets and intellectual property may involve:

- Platform-specific designation updates
- Custodian documentation
- Contractual coordination

Digital asset governance may differ from traditional property alignment.

Security credentials and access information should be maintained separately from trust documentation.

PART VII — PERIODIC REVIEW CONTEXT

Implementation may be revisited due to:

- Changes in family structure
- Asset acquisition or divestment
- Regulatory developments
- Trustee succession
- Evolving beneficiary circumstances

Periodic review supports coherence.
It does not imply required amendment.

Structural Reminder

Execution and funding are implementation functions governed by:

- Applicable law
- Trust classification
- Asset category
- Institutional procedure

This Appendix provides governance awareness — not procedural instruction.

APPENDIX D — COMPARATIVE TRUST MATRIX

(Structural Reference Overview)

Purpose

This Appendix presents a comparative overview of governance distinctions discussed throughout this guide.

The matrix format clarifies:

- Governance contrasts
- Depth of authority separation
- Distribution design variation
- Administrative layering
- Architectural tradeoffs

This Appendix provides comparison — not recommendation.

PART I — REVOCABLE VS IRREVOCABLE FRAMEWORKS

Structural Element	Revocable Framework	Irrevocable Framework
Amendment Authority	Generally retained by Grantor	Generally restricted or unavailable
Grantor Control	Retained during lifetime	Typically relinquished or limited
Trustee Independence	Often unified with Grantor	Typically independent
Structural Permanence	Flexible	Intended to be enduring

Governance Emphasis	Administrative continuity	Long-term fiduciary governance
Structural Orientation	Adaptable	Disciplined and defined

The primary distinction centers on retained authority and governance independence.

PART II — GRANTOR-ORIENTED VS NON-GRANTOR-ORIENTED STRUCTURES

(Conceptual Overview)

Conceptual Feature	Grantor-Oriented Structure	Non-Grantor-Oriented Structure
Administrative Control	May remain centralized	Typically separated
Income Treatment (Conceptual)	May be associated with Grantor	May be treated independently
Governance Model	Consolidated	Independent fiduciary
Structural Intent	Flexibility	Separation and permanence

Tax classification is determined by governing law and drafting precision — not by conceptual labels alone.

PART III — SIMPLE VS LAYERED DISTRIBUTION STRUCTURES

Distribution Dimension	Simplified Model	Layered / Complex Model
Distribution Timing	Direct or periodic	Multi-tiered or staged
Trustee Discretion	Limited	Structured or broad
Beneficiary Conditions	Minimal	Standard-based or milestone-based
Administrative Oversight	Straightforward	Governance-intensive

Distribution architecture often determines the long-term behavioral character of a trust.

PART IV — GOVERNANCE DEPTH COMPARISON

(Foundational vs Expanded Design)

Governance Dimension	Foundational Structure	Expanded Governance Structure
Core Articles	Direct application	Expanded with specialized provisions
Governance Layers	Minimal	Multi-layered
Asset Scope	Generalized	Asset-specific

Distribution Design	Simplified	Nuanced or staged
Trustee Hierarchy	Limited	Defined succession hierarchy
Administrative Safeguards	Basic	Enhanced

Expanded governance adds layering — it does not replace foundational architecture.

PART V — TRUST TYPE CHARACTERISTICS (AT A GLANCE)

Trust Type	Primary Objective	Governance Orientation	Distribution Emphasis
Revocable	Flexibility & organization	Unified	Adaptive
Irrevocable	Structural independence	Fiduciary	Defined
Family	Intergenerational stewardship	Discretion-based	Balanced
Spendthrift	Protective oversight	Trustee-centered	Controlled
Charitable	Purpose-defined	Mission-focused	Structured
Land	Title structuring	Administrative	Ownership-based

Business-Holding	Ownership continuity	Coordinated governance	Succession-focused
Intellectual Property	Intangible asset continuity	Rights-focused	Royalty-based
Special Needs	Supplemental support	Discretionary	Needs-based
Education	Purpose-restricted funding	Criteria-based	Defined
Firearms	Compliance-oriented governance	Regulatory-aware	Structured succession
Digital Asset	Access continuity	Authority-coordinated	Governance-stability

Trust type reflects governance orientation — not inherent advantage.

Structural Reminder

Comparative matrices simplify complex legal architecture.

Legal classification, tax treatment, enforceability, and fiduciary standards depend on:

- Governing jurisdiction
- Drafting precision
- Asset composition
- Administrative conduct

This Appendix provides structural literacy only.

Why This Appendix Matters

Trust governance can feel abstract without visual comparison.

A structured matrix:

- Clarifies architectural contrasts
- Distinguishes flexibility from permanence
- Highlights governance layering
- Illustrates distribution tradeoffs
- Reinforces structural literacy

Comparison strengthens conceptual confidence.

APPENDIX E — FUTURE PLANNING CONSIDERATIONS

(Long-Term Governance Commentary)

Purpose

Trust planning is rarely static.

Over time, personal circumstances, asset composition, fiduciary capacity, and legal environments evolve.

This Appendix addresses long-term governance alignment beyond initial formation. It is forward-looking and reflective — not prescriptive.

PART I — MULTI-GENERATIONAL CONTINUITY

Some trust structures operate primarily during a lifetime. Others are designed for generational durability.

Long-term considerations may include:

- Preservation of principal across decades
- Distribution philosophy for future descendants
- Trustee succession beyond original appointees
- Governance resilience over time

Sustained continuity requires balancing flexibility with structural discipline.

PART II — DIGITAL ASSET EVOLUTION

Digital assets may increase in technical complexity, regulatory exposure, and custodial variation over time.

Forward-looking considerations include:

- Changes in custody models
- Regulatory developments
- Platform governance shifts
- Integration with traditional asset structures

Digital governance benefits from periodic reassessment.

Security credentials and authentication controls should remain operationally separate from trust documentation.

PART III — BUSINESS SUCCESSION DEVELOPMENT

Closely held business interests often evolve materially.

Long-term coordination may involve:

- Expansion or transfer of ownership interests
- Introduction of new partners or stakeholders
- Amendments to operating or shareholder agreements
- Intergenerational leadership transition

Trust structures holding business interests function most effectively when aligned with governing entity documents.

Ownership governance and operational governance must remain coordinated.

PART IV — BENEFICIARY LIFE STAGES

Beneficiaries change across time.

Governance awareness may include:

- Transition from minority to adulthood
- Development of financial literacy
- Emergence of special circumstances
- Changes in education, career, or residency

Distribution philosophy may benefit from periodic review to maintain alignment with original intent.

PART V — ADAPTABILITY & STRUCTURAL LIMITATIONS

Certain developments arise unpredictably:

- Health changes
- Jurisdictional relocation
- Marriage or divorce
- Regulatory shifts
- Asset volatility

Some trust frameworks accommodate modification.
Others prioritize permanence and restrict amendment authority.

Responsible governance requires understanding structural boundaries before change becomes necessary.

PART VI — PERIODIC REVIEW CONTEXT

Periodic review supports alignment.

Illustrative review triggers may include:

- Major life events
- Significant asset changes
- Trustee succession
- Regulatory developments

Review does not imply amendment.
It reinforces continuity.

PART VII — STEWARDSHIP & INTENT

Trust planning is governance by design.

Long-term stewardship may involve:

- Preservation of values alongside assets
- Clear articulation of intent
- Continuity of fiduciary responsibility
- Balance between protection and empowerment

Trusts are structural tools.
Their impact depends on alignment between purpose, drafting, administration, and oversight.

Closing Reflection

Future planning considerations are influenced by:

- Governing law
- Regulatory environment
- Asset classification
- Beneficiary development
- Trustee capacity

Trust planning extends beyond document execution.

It represents governance architecture across time.

Forward-looking awareness may:

- Strengthen durability
- Reduce administrative disruption
- Support generational continuity
- Preserve alignment between intent and implementation

This Appendix reinforces stewardship and continuity — not static completion.

FINAL NOTES & NEXT STEPS

(Closing Perspective)

Before You Close This Guide

If you have reached this point, you have already taken the most important step:

You chose understanding before implementation.

Deliberate planning begins with literacy — not paperwork.

What This Guide Was Designed to Provide

This guide was written to help you:

- Understand trust structure at its architectural core
- Recognize how roles, authority, and governance interact
- Compare revocable and irrevocable frameworks without pressure
- See how structural concepts translate into written language
- Reflect on continuity, distribution philosophy, and fiduciary design

It was not designed to compel action.

It was designed to clarify.

There Is No Deadline Attached to Understanding

Trust literacy develops in stages.

You are not expected to:

- Finalize documents immediately
- Select a framework under urgency
- Transfer assets prematurely
- Resolve every structural question at once

Reflection is not delay.
 It is disciplined preparation.

When — and If — You Choose to Move Forward

For some readers, next steps may include:

- Revisiting sections for deeper clarity
- Comparing governance models side by side
- Discussing architecture with qualified advisors
- Aligning trust design with long-term objectives

There is no universal sequence.

Each path is shaped by circumstance, jurisdiction, and intent.

The Value of Professional Perspective

Trust instruments may carry lasting legal and financial implications.

Professional review may strengthen:

- Jurisdictional alignment
- Drafting precision
- Structural coherence
- Asset coordination
- Administrative continuity

Understanding structure enhances collaboration.
It does not replace expertise.

A Living Reference

This guide is intended to function as an architectural reference.

Many readers return to it:

- After significant life changes
- Before advisory conversations
- When evaluating trustee roles
- When reconsidering distribution philosophy
- When reassessing governance structure

It is not a checklist.

It is a framework for clarity.

Closing Perspective

Trust structures are not ultimately about documents.

They are about:

- Intentional governance
- Defined authority
- Continuity across time
- Stewardship of responsibility

Documents record structure.
Understanding gives structure legitimacy.

End of Guide